My Life

at

Speke Hall

By
Tom Whatmore

First Edition: September 1993
Second Edition: January 1994

Third Edition: Revised and re-set January 2009

This edition published 2009 by Countyvise Limited,
14 Appin Road, Birkenhead, Wirral CH41 9HH.

British Library Cataloguing in Publication Data.
A catalogue record for this book is available from the British Library.

ISBN 978 1 906823 1 77

The 'Whatmore' Family
1926, South Front

Contents

INTRODUCTION

All the books published on the history of Speke Hall stop at the death of Miss Adelaide Watt, but the Hall and its history continued. What I have tried to do is mainly to record what took place during the period 1920 to 1946 at the Hall, on the estate and in the township of Speke.

During this time a lot of history was made which up to this date has not been recorded.

After the death of Miss Watt in 1921, the lives of the retainers and their families were part of that history. My family's life was also part of that history.

I have tried to record their lives at the Hall, what it meant to them, and the way their being at the Hall affected my life. By writing this book I hope to fix their names in its history. What I have written is all fact. I have come to that time of life when the past, if not recorded, will slip away and be forgotten. This would be a great shame for all those people who played their part in keeping the Hall as it is today.

The early history must also play its part, so I make no apologies for including this, although it has been written about many times in the past. It did affect my life at the Hall and, therefore, formed part of my growing up, so I have recounted the parts I feel are relevant and of interest to the reader.

As I am the last of the people left alive who lived in the Hall during this period (as far as I know) the task of writing this history is mine. I hope that by doing this the names of the old retainers and workers of the estate will be remembered.

I trust that what I have written will be of interest to the reader and to my family, who have encouraged me to research, and to do a lot of deep thinking and work to compile this book. My only regret is that my father and brother are now dead and will not see the result. I also regret that I did not ask my father more questions during his life; his answers would have made the writing much easier.

My apologies to any one I have left out who feels that they should have been mentioned. I hope you will forgive any omissions, and enjoy any part that is remembered.

I have now included in the latest edition of my book, the history of the Church, Church School, the account of parish activities, the building of Speke Airport, the housing estate, and the factory estate, the alterations to the Speke countryside. Information relating to these matters was all taken from the Speke Church Parochial Annual of 1930 to 1938.

The account of Speke Hall Home Farm is based on my personal knowledge of the farm and its buildings.

I have tried to mention all the families that had any part in the history, running or organising of the many activities in the Speke Township.

For the history of the different families I have to thank the present day descendants and any with connections to these families for their stories and accounts of the different happenings in and around the estate.

I have now also added an extra chapter 'The Nearly Completed Circle'. This chapter continues from 1946 to 2008 with my returning to the Hall after my absence of some 40 years and what is happening to nearly complete the circle.

I trust that these extra chapters will be of interest to any descendants of the old population of the Speke Township.

Tom Whatmore, November 2008

CHAPTER 1
THE STORY STARTS HERE

My life started at the Hall in 1922, but my story starts long before that. Speke Hall was first recorded in the Domesday Book of 1086, which states that, the 'Manor of Spec' had been held by Uctred or Uchtred since 1066, and possibly from some earlier date. Uctred was a Saxon thane of some considerable consequence, who appears to have enjoyed a much greater measure of freedom and property than was usually accorded to the thanes under Norman rule.

By 1200 the tenure of the Manor of Speke was held by the Molyneux Family, through marriage to the families of De Hasewal and the Erneys of Chester. In 1314 John and Nicola Norris, through marriage into these families, occupied a house, which stood on, or adjacent to the site now accommodating Speke Hall.

In 1367 the Hall was in the hands of John Le Norris who had succeeded in 1350. Sir William Norris I succeeded to the Manor of Speke in 1490 and initiated the building of the present Hall. Sir William Norris II carried out further alterations. In about 1535 he had the Great Hall divided with a partition, technically called the screens.

About 1560 during the time of Sir William II, the west side of the house was completed. The north side was completed in 1598 for Edward Norris. A chapel was incorporated in this block and was called the 'New Chapel', which replaced the 'Old Chapel' in the West Wing.

By 1736 the Hall was in the hands of the Beauclerk family, and by 1795 it had been sold to Richard Watt I.

This was the house that my brother and I grew up in, with all its history. I am going to start my story with the Watt family, for without them we would not have lived at Speke Hall.

The first Richard Watt was born at Shevington, Standish in 1724. As a young man he drove a hire carriage in Liverpool for a Mr Geoffrey Walley, who sent him to evening school in Liverpool, and in 1750 employed him to go to Jamaica as a super-cargo. This was a person employed on a merchant ship to manage sales of cargo.

1

Whilst in Jamaica he amassed a fortune in the region of £500,000 and returned to Liverpool some forty years later to do extensive trade with the West Indies.

In 1795 he purchased Speke Hall and its estate from Charles George Beauclerk for the sum of £75,500. The Hall had suffered a great deal of neglect in the 18th century while it was in the hands of the Beauclerk family. Watt would then have been according to records, aged 71 years. It is said that he only lived for one year after the purchase of the Hall and died at the age of 72 years.

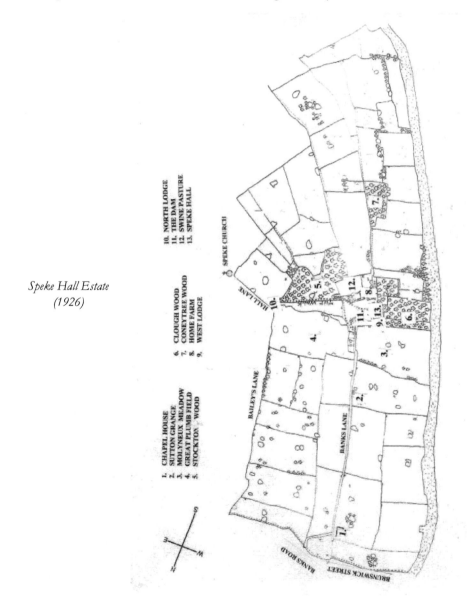

Speke Hall Estate
(1926)

1. CHAPEL HOUSE
2. SUTTON GRANGE
3. MOLYNEUX MEADOW
4. GREAT PLUMB FIELD
5. STOCKTON WOOD

6. CLOUGH WOOD
7. CONEYTREE WOOD
8. HOME FARM
9. WEST LODGE

10. NORTH LODGE
11. THE DAM
12. SWINE PASTURE
13. SPEKE HALL

As he died without issue, his fortune and estate in Speke passed to his kinsman, Richard Watt of Bishop Burton, East Yorkshire.

This Richard Watt died in 1803 and left the Hall to his son, another Richard Watt, and so on through future Richard Watts until 1865 when the last Richard Watt the fifth died in tragic circumstances. There are various accounts of how he met his death.

The Greyhound

It is said that he was in the habit of frequenting the local hostelry, letting his horse bring him home after his evening's merry making. One night in 1865 he must have fallen asleep, tumbled off his cart, under the wheel and was killed. The one local hostelry was the 'Greyhound' in Butchers Lane Speke. Miss Watt closed the inn in 1878.

It is also said that he was sailing on the Mersey on his yacht the 'Goshawk', fell overboard, and was drowned. Neither of these stories is true.

On the 9th December 1865 he was in the Isle of Wight at Cowes sailing his yacht the 'Goshawk'. He fell over the side and was drowned. Whichever way he died, his death was doubly tragic because he was only thirty years old and already a widower.

LIVERPOOL WEEKLY NEWS   **DECEMBER 11ᵀᴴ 1865**

FUNERAL OF THE LATE RICHARD WATT, ESQ.

The obsequies of the late Richard Watt, Esq. of Speke Hall, took place on Thursday at the Old Church of St Michael, Garston. As already announced in our obituary, the deceased died, after a few weeks' illness on Saturday last, at West Cowes, Isle of Wight. He was in his 30ᵗʰ year.

The body was brought to Liverpool by railway on Monday evening, and, under the direction of two of the relatives, conveyed thence in a hearse to the family mansion, at Speke. So far as the relatives of the deceased were concerned, the funeral was conducted in as private a manner as possible.

The funeral 'cortege' left the residence of the deceased shortly after twelve o'clock and comprised a hearse, seven mourning coaches, and several private carriages, besides a number of tenantry resident on the estate. The tenantry and officials connected with the mansion, attired in deep mourning, were drawn up on each side of the courtyard, the body of the deceased being borne down the centre on its way to the hearse.

The family and friends followed, and on the carriages being occupied the mournful equipage was formed, and proceeded to the place of interment.

In advance of the hearse were the tenantry, headed by Mr J. Meredith, of Vineyard, Garston, land steward to the late Mr Watt. Following the hearse came the chief mourners in two carriages. The first carriage contained Captain Watt, uncle to the deceased; Rev, Mr. Hudson, his brother-in-law; Mrs Gardner, his mother; and Mrs. Hudson, the deceased's sister. In the second carriage were F. Hignett, Esq, father of the late Mrs Watt; W. Hignett, Esq, Miss Gardner, and Miss Bland. Third carriage: C. S. Starkie Esq, W. D. Evans Esq, Lieutenant Colonel Blackburne (of Hale), Alfred Fletcher Esq. Fourth carriage: G. Whitley Esq, Joseph Miller, Esq, Rev. J. Gibson (incumbent of Garston Church), and the Rev. H. Jones.

The fifth, sixth and seventh carriages were occupied by the officials connected with the Hall, the rear being brought up by four private carriages, those of J. I. Blackburne, Esq, of Hale Hall; A. Fletcher, Esq; G. Stone, Esq of Liverpool (who occupied his own vehicle); and J. Wharton, Esq of Garston.

At each side of the carriages walked, at certain distances, 16 men employed on the Speke Hall estate. Others were also placed near the hearse, officiating as under bearers. When the mournful procession left the Hall a number of persons assembled as spectators of the ceremony, and others followed during the route. There was also a numerous gathering at the church. The Rev. J. Gibson read the burial service, the incumbent assisted by the Rev. H. Jones. The remains of the deceased were deposited in the family vault, inside the church, in front of the altar, where the late Mrs Watt was interred about three years ago.

The coffin covered with black cloth and elegantly mounted with brass, bore a solid silver shield on which was inscribed- "Richard Watt; born October 25, 1835; died December 9, 1865".

The funeral service being concluded, the relatives and friends of the deceased took a final look in the vault and then retired from the church. The carriages having been re-arranged returned direct to the Hall. Messrs, Wheelwright and Co, of Bold Street, had the conduct of the funeral arrangements, which were carried out in every respect most satisfactorily.

The above article about the funeral rites of Richard V was taken from a copy of the *Liverpool Weekly News*, written at that time. It states that Mrs. Jane Gardner is the mother of Richard Watt V, this is correct. Jane remarried Richard Gardner a man of independent means in 1847, after the death of Richard Watt IV. In 1835 (Richard V's father). Miss Gardner is the daughter of Jane and Richard Gardner.

Miss Bland has some connection with Jane as her maiden name was Bland before she married Richard Watt IV.

Jane was born in 1824 and died on 6th October 1888; she would then have been 64/65 years old. It is interesting to note that Jane was at the 21st birthday party of the granddaughter, Adelaide on the 21st May 1878. Miss Gardner was also there.

Richard V was placed in the vault of the second church of Garston under the chancel floor. The first church or chapel had been built in about 1255 and it was then referred to as St Wilfred. It was found in ruins in 1650; no services had been held in it for many years.

The second church dedicated to St Michael, was built for Edward Norris with £300 left by his mother for this purpose and an extra £60 from himself. This church was built in 1715 on the same site as the first church.

In the summer of 1874 a faculty was obtained for the demolition of the old church and the building of a new one on the same site. The foundation stone was laid on the 18th May 1875 and was consecrated on the 29th November 1877. This was the third church on the site.

The first vicar of the new church from 1875 to 1884 was the Rev John Fitzgerald Hewson. His wife was Sara Watt a sister to Richard V and Aunt to Adelaide Watt.

In the west end of the present church there are monuments to Edward Norris erected by his wife Anne. In addition there is one to Richard Watt IV and one to Richard Watt V, his wife Adelaide and daughter Edith. These monuments were first in the chancel of the second church, which was demolished in 1874.

Also in the present church there are two hatchments, one of these represents the Beauclerk family, the other the Watt family. These hatchments were also originally in the chancel of the second church.

In the churchyard on the west of the church is a gravestone with the Norris family crest on it.

The Hall then passed to his daughter Adelaide, who was only 8 years old. She was born on the 20th May 1857 in Scotland. Her sister Edith, born in May 1859, only lived nine days and her mother Adelaide (nee Highett), died on the 8th August 1861 in Kinross, Scotland, after a short illness, aged only 23 years.

After her father's death Adelaide was put under the guardianship of her uncle, Mr. James Sprot of Dunbar, Scotland and the Hall was leased to the Leyland family. During their tenancy they carried out many repairs and renovations to the Hall.

THE NEW CHURCH AT SPEKE

All Saints Church Speke was built for Miss Watt by order of her guardian Mr. James Sprot at a cost of £7,000. The foundation stone was laid on the 1st November 1872 by Miss Watt (this stone is now inside the new vestry built in 1939.) The architect was Mr. W Pearson, and no expense was spared. The red sandstone for the building came from the quarry at Delph Lane. It was built in the Gothic style, with low pointed arches and perpendicular windows with geometric designs in the tracery. Doors and pews were made of oak, with seating for 200 persons.

All Saints Church, Speke

Gavel and trowel

CEREMONY IN CONNECTION WITH THE 'ORDER OF SERVICE' TO BE OBSERVED ON THE OCCASION OF LAYING THE 'FOUNDATION STONE' OF THE CHURCH OF ALL SAINTS SPEKE. AT 12.45am. 1st NOVEMBER 1872:

The visitors being assembled into their places leaving a clear space around the foundation stone. Some of the principal tenantry will proceed to the entrance of the ground and on the entrance of Miss Watt will escort her in procession to the stone.

PROCESSION

The Architect with plans	
The Phial with coins	Coins by Mr. Whitley
The Level	Borne by Mr. Charlton
The Cornucopia with corn	
The Vessel with wine	
The Vessel with oil	
The Bible (open)	Borne by The Chaplain
The Trowel	Borne by Mr. Byron
The Mallet	Borne by Mr. Mawdsley

Mrs. Sprot   Miss Watt   Mr. Sprot
Gentlemen two and two

Having arrived at the Stone, a hymn will be sung, and prayers offered, after which a psalm will be chanted. The Apostles' Creed said.

The phial containing the coins will then be placed in the cavity in the Stone and cement laid upon the Stone.

The Trowel will then be presented to Miss Watt, who will spread the cement. The Stone will then be lowered to its bed. (Solemn music being played). The Stone being placed Miss Watt will try if the stone is properly adjusted by means of the level, which will be handed to her for that purpose.

The mallet will then be presented to Miss Watt who will give **three** distinct knocks therewith upon the Stone, saying 'In the faith of our Lord Jesus Christ we lay this foundation Stone to the glory of God the Father, God the Son, and God the Holy Ghost, Amen.'

The vessel containing corn will be handed to Miss Watt who will place some upon the Stone. The Chaplain saying 'Corn the emblem of plenty, may God the Father endow us plenteously with His blessing'.

The vessel containing wine will then be handed to Miss Watt who will pour some of it upon the Stone, the Chaplain saying 'Wine the emblem of Grace and Truth may God the Son grant us his heavenly Grace to guide us in the way of Truth'.

The vessel with oil will then be handed to Miss Watt, who will pour some upon the Stone, the Chaplain saying 'Oil the emblem of Peace and goodwill. May God the Holy Ghost in His infinite goodness and mercy speedily fulfill our Saviour's promise of peace on Earth and goodwill towards men.

Then follows the Collect and prayers and a hymn will be sung.

The Architect then delivers the plans to Miss Watt who (having approved of them) hands them to the Builder, desiring him to proceed with the building without delay.

Concluding with the Blessing.

The Peace.

At 21 years of age on 20th May 1878 Miss Watt took over the full possession of Speke Hall. On this day two parties were held to celebrate her coming of age, one for her close friends and relations and one for the inside and outside staff, retainers and others.

The first of these dinner parties was held at five o'clock on the lawn. This was for about 80 guests, tenants and their families.

The other party in the evening was for the cottagers of the estate. They were entertained in a marquee in a field adjoining the lawn.

To celebrate the occasion, the workers and retainers presented Miss Watt with an address in book form, which consisted of several pages of illuminated manuscript, surrounded by conventionally treated floral borders and containing portraits of Miss Watt, Mr. Sprot and Mr. Whitley; as well as two views of Speke Hall. The work was handsomely bound in crimson morocco, richly tooled and lined inside with white water silk.

The armorial bearings of Miss Watt appeared in the work and on the outside, surrounded by a richly engraved plate, double gilt, burnished and saw-pierced. The volume, which was prepared by Mr. James. O. Marples was enclosed in a case made of oak, grown on the estate and lined with purple velvet.

Miss Adelaide Watt
at 21 years

It is recorded in the *Liverpool Mercury* of Tuesday May 21st 1878 that Miss Watt presented her two trustees, Mr. Sprot and Mr. Whitley each with a beautiful silver cup on behalf of the tenantry of the estate. She said on this occasion: *"I feel proud that the Speke tenantry have given me this opportunity of showing how they appreciate the conduct of these two gentlemen I am so much indebted to."* After her 21st birthday Miss Watt spent the greater part of her life at Speke Hall.

Under the expert guidance of her uncle, Mr. Sprot, she learned how to be "Lady of the Manor" and how to control the Speke estate.

It is recorded that she was People's Warden of All Saints Church, Speke until her death in 1921. During her life she had also a strong connection with St. Michael's Church, Garston.

In 1888 it is recorded that she had contentions with the contractors who were building a boundary wall at Garston Church and it was not until April 1889 that the work was resumed and completed. The cost for this work was met by Miss Watt, after having the sum collected by the Vicar and others, and paid into her account. This sum was £250.

Work was done on the boundary wall, a lych-gate and the approach to the church in Church Road. Miss Watt, being patroness of the living, had undertaken to build the wall on condition that the stones and materials of the old church were used.

Garston Church boundary wall

The Coronation of Edward VII on the 6th September 1902 was celebrated at the Hall.

A description of the festivities was reported in the local newspaper of that date, Sometime before her death, during the building of Liverpool Cathedral, Miss Watt gave a sum of £1250 for a Bishop's Throne in the Cathedral in memory

9

of Richard Watt I. *"A Citizen of Liverpool 1724-1796"* is the phrase she had engraved.

When in 1920 my father went to Speke Hall as butler to Miss Watt, she was then 63 years old. Living with her at the Hall at this time was her aunt, Mrs. Anne Starkie, her cousin Mrs. Charlotte Smithson (nee Starkie) and a friend and companion, a Miss Janet Lee-Steere (the latter two died in 1938).

When she died on the 21st August 1921 at the age of 64 years she was the last of her line. 126 years of the Watts at Speke Hall have left their mark. Without their money and interest Speke Hall would have been left derelict and in ruins.

THE TRUST

Miss Watt left Speke Hall in trust for 21 years for Mr. Richard Stanley Fitzgerald Hewson and then for the Norris family. She left an estate of £321,000.14s.1d gross and £183,573.16s.2d nett. The trustees were Dr Foxley Norris (died 1937), Rev Edward John Norris and a Mr. Powlett.

Also included in this will is the stipulation that whoever took over the Hall after the 21 years trust, had to insert "Watt" before their surname. (In the case of Mr. R. S. F. Hewson to replace his present or any other surname.) Mr. Hewson negotiated with the National Trust in 1943, so declining to use "Watt" as his name. Thus he forfeited his right to the Estate. Any other person also had to use Watt instead of or with and before or after his or her present surname. They also had to use and continue to use the arms of Watt or quarter the same with their own family arms. Thus it passed to the Norris family, who had no hesitation in including Watt in their name.

On a visit to East Riddlesden Hall, Keighley, West Yorkshire, I was shown a copy of the family tree of the Murgatroyd and Starkie families. These families owned the East Riddlesden Hall from 1600s to the 1800s. On examination I noted the marriage of an Alice Norris and a Mary Foxley. Both these names have a connection with Speke Hall.

James Murgatroyd built East Riddlesden Hall, but in 1653 a Mary Murgatroyd married a Nicholas Starkie of Huntroyde, Nr Padiham, Burnley. Their son John married an Alice Norris on the 21st October 1654, and their fifth son William married a Mary Foxley c1670.

In 1753 a Mr. Thomas Le Gendre, a rich London draper, descended from the Huguenot family, left money in his will to "my friend Nicholas Starkie, and to his son John now to become Le Gendre Starkie £500 in trust until he shall attain the age of 21 years." So the name "Le Gendre" came into the Starkie name.

Alice Norris born in 1635 was a descendant of Sir Henry Norris and Alice Erneys of Speke Hall on the Blackrod, Bolton side of the family. [From Edward Norris and Dorothy Brettergh of Park Hall, Blackrod, Bolton c1540, to Alexander Norris c1546, to Alice Norris and Christopher of Tonge-with Haulgh, Bolton c1600, to Anne and Alexander of Hall in The Wood c1620.] Hall in The Wood was a 15th century half-timbered manor house and was part of her marriage settlement.

In 1779 William Norris MD married Deborah Foxley, William was also a descendant of Sir Henry Norris and Alice Erneys, and Edward and Dorothy of Park Hall, Bolton. In 1650 a Norris of this branch of the family went to Ireland and had three sons. One of these sons, William, subsequently settled in Bolton. William of Limerick had a son John, born 1719, who, in 1741, married Ann Causer. One of his sons was William Norris MD born 1748.

This branch of the Norris family now added Foxley to the family name in 1824, and from this branch in 1915 Michael was born and in 1917 Christopher. Michael became one of the trustees of Speke Hall in the 1930s.

In 1795 Speke Hall was sold to Richard Watt I and by 1878 the owner was Adelaide Watt. Charlotte Watt was Adelaide's aunt, and in 1834 she married Harrington Hudson, of Bessington York. Their daughter Anne Charlotte Amelia married John P. C. Starkie of Ashton Hall, (between Lancaster and Cockerham on the River Lune) in 1861. John Piers Chamberlain Starkie was a brother to Le Gendre Nicholas Starkie of Huntroyde, heir to Riddlesden Hall.

Thus we have a connection between the Norris, Foxley, Starkie and the Watt families. In Adelaide's will of the 23rd May 1919 she stipulates that Watt should be added to the name of whoever became entitled to the Hall after the trust period. The Norris family eventually took over the ownership of the Hall and added Watt into their name. Thus the Foxley Norris's became Foxley Watt Norris.

I wonder if Adelaide knew of this connection when she had her Will made in 1919?

Miss Watt was cremated and her ashes are buried in All Saints Church Speke on the left hand side of the altar. By 1926 the Hall had become empty and according to Miss Watt's will it was to be held in trust for 21 years. The trustees therefore asked my father if he would move into Speke Hall with his family as caretaker to complete the trust. He agreed to do this and kept any agreement meticulously.

In 1942 Mr. Hewson entered into negotiations with the National Trust and Speke Hall became their property in 1943.

A letter appeared in the local newspaper in 1943 from Mr. Hewson under the heading, 'Acquisition of Speke Hall':

"Sir, I have only presently had sent to me a cutting from (I believe) your issue of July 22nd last, re the acquisition by Liverpool Corporation of Speke Hall, and headed "Mansion in Liverpool Possession".

I should like to draw attention and that of your readers to an error in the last paragraph, in which it is stated that by Miss Ada Watt's will, the property passed to the modern descendants of the Norris family. This is not correct.

My cousin Miss Adelaide Watt, when she died in 1921, left the estate in trust for the benefit of myself and certain of the Norris family for twenty-one years, at the end of which period the estate was to be held in trust for me during my lifetime.

The twenty-one years expired in August last year. I am still in the land of the living and recently gave my consent and approval to the negotiations with the National Trust.

Yours, &C, R. S. Fitzgerald Hewson,
7 Somerhill Court, Holland Road, Hove."

In the Magazine of St Michael's Parish Church Garston of September 1921, it says: *"On Sunday, August 21st, at 3-45pm, Adelaide Watt of Speke Hall, Lancashire and Spott House, Haddingtonshire passed peacefully away into the unseen world at the age of 64".* It goes on to say that for several years she had been in failing health but the end came with almost tragic suddenness.

On Saturday morning she appeared much as usual but about noon she complained of feeling unwell. The doctor was called and on Sunday morning the specialist. At about 3 pm The Rev Canon Rowe, Vicar of Garston, held a Commendatory Service. On St Bartholomew's Day a Memorial Eucharist was held at Speke Church, followed by cremation at Anfield and on Thursday August 25th an impressive service took place when the "ashes" of Adelaide Watt were laid in the sanctuary; the officiating clergy being the Rev. L .R. Paterson. Vicar of Speke, the Rev. Canon Rowe, Vicar of Garston, and the Rev. J. D. Bruce, Vicar of Dunbar. The Dean of York, Venerable Foxley Norris, was among the congregation.

It also says that Miss Watt lived a secluded life and mingled little in Society, being engrossed in the management of her large estates in which she took the most profound interest. Nobody could possibly have worked harder or more conscientiously, most of the hours of every day being spent in dealing with her voluminous correspondence.

Nobody who knew her could ever forget her charming personality, her delicious speaking voice, her keen intellect, her cultured even ascetic countenance, her spare form, bowed and burdened with the weight of the immense responsibility of the administration of her large estates

Adelaide Watt
circa 1920

THE WHATMORE FAMILY

My father, Thomas Whatmore, was born on the 30th May 1880 and his birth was registered at Bewdley near Kidderminster. As a boy of 13 years of age he was employed by the Woodward family in Arley Castle, Arley, near Kidderminster as a pageboy. This is a boy in livery employed to attend to the door and go on errands. He progressed to be a footman by 1908, at Gwysaney Hall, Mold, North Wales. The footman is a liveried servant for carriage, door and table. By 1912 he was a valet, in the employ of the Baldwin family at Astly Hall, Dunley, which overlooks the river Severn. The valet is a manservant who attends on person and clothes. In the servants' hierarchy the valet was numbered among the so-called 'Upper Ten'.

He enlisted in the King's Shropshire Light Infantry on the 6th December 1915. His civil occupation was listed as valet. In the army he was employed as an officer's cook and was demobilised on the 13th March 1919. His army number was 23731.

On the 1st October 1916 he married Mary Griffiths of Leominster at the Parish Church of Tettenhall, Stafford. Mary Griffiths was at that time the cook at the Wood House, Tettenhall. Her birth was on the 17th March 1888. In 1919 after the First World War he came to Liverpool with his wife, and lived in 9 Verulan Street off Parliament Street, and held

Mary (Polly) Whatmore (nee Griffiths)

13

the position of butler, the servant in charge, in the household of Henry Sutton Timmis of 4, Croxteth Road, Liverpool. During his time there my brother Frank was born on the 6th February 1920.

Sometime in 1920 he left Croxteth Road and went to Speke Hall as butler to Miss Adelaide Watt. He and his family lived in the end four rooms of the Home Farm's house with the bailiff (land-steward) and his wife, Mr and Mrs George L. Wilkin. On the 11th May 1922 I was born in this farmhouse and later christened Thomas William Whatmore.

Part of Home Farm Bailiff's Farmhouse

West Lodge (1924)

14

On the 21st August 1921 Miss Watt died and my father became butler to Mrs. Anne Starkie. Mrs. Starkie was Miss Watt's aunt and was living in Speke Hall at that time with her daughter, Mrs. Smithson and companion Miss Lee Steere. By 1924 we had moved into the West Lodge. The household at the Hall continued to work just as it had done during Miss Watt's time. Then in 1926 things changed, all the inside staff were given notice and the Hall was closed.

My first recollection of going into Speke Hall was in 1924 when I was about two years old. I was taken by my father to see the kitchen staff and was given a scone by the cook. I can remember the kitchen being full of people and a very busy place.

It was in 1926 that my father was asked by the trustees of the estate to become caretaker of Speke Hall for the rest of the 21 years of the Trust. Thus as a family we moved into the Hall. By this time Mrs. Starkie, Mrs. Smithson and Miss Lee-Steere had left the Hall. We can presume that Mrs. Smithson did not live in the Hall after 1925 because her parting gift to my father was a book, *The Pilgrimages to Old Homes* by Fletcher Moss. It is inscribed as follows:

"To Whatmore in memory of Speke Days from Mrs. Smithson 1925"

When we first moved into the Hall we had use of the following rooms on the ground floor: The kitchen, scullery, larders, butler's pantry, housekeeper's room, and the 'Blue Drawing Room'.

Kitchen range

In the kitchen my mother had to cook on the 1916 range for the first year or so, but eventually a smaller range was installed for us in the butler's pantry.

On the first floor, in the old servants' quarters, we had our bedrooms. These rooms were over the kitchen.

During Miss Watt's life at the Hall she had central heating installed (in 1895), hot and cold water supplies, flush toilets and a telephone (number Garston 131) but the Hall was lit solely by oil lamps until 1934-35. In this way our family started its life in Speke Hall.

The arrangements the trustees made with my father were that he would be paid a salary, plus coal, coke, oil for lighting and vegetables from the gardens. A sum per annum was allowed for seed. The gardeners were to be allowed any surplus vegetables. In addition supplies were to be sent to Speke Church at harvest time.

Tom Whatmore
'Private' (1916)

Tom Whatmore
'Page Boy' (1894)

Frank and Tom Whatmore South Front (1933)

17

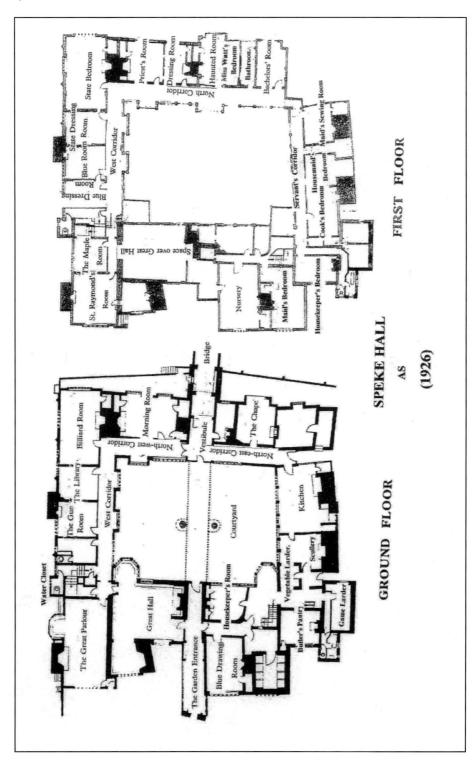

SPEKE HALL
AS
(1926)

FIRST FLOOR

GROUND FLOOR

CHAPTER 2
SPEKE HALL: 'OUR HOME'

'Our Home'

Speke Hall was our home for 20 years. We grew up to think of it as such. All of its rooms were open to us and many of them hold memories for me.

It was my father's job to see that the inside of the Hall was maintained to the same standard as during the life of the last owner Miss Adelaide Watt. The rooms were not cocooned in dustsheets. It was one of my father's duties to organise the

19

cleaning into a weekly routine, from Monday to Friday. The rooms, galleries, and corridors were dusted. The wooden floors were polished with the brand 'O' cedar oil and the stone floors washed.

During the years 1926 to 1942 we had many visitors, who came with permission either of the trustees or my father. Visitors always started their tour at the north entrance, so I am also going to start my tour from here to the rooms and places that have a memory for me.

THIS WORKE 25 YARDS LONG, WAS WHOLLY BUILT BY EDW.N. ESQ. A.N.D. 1598.

These are the words over the main entrance of Speke Hall. 'This Worke' was, at one time, thought to refer to the bridge spanning the moat, but as the north block measures almost exactly 25 yards long between the east and west blocks, it would appear that it refers to the north block.

Water Colour of Speke Hall Before (1598), by Tom Whatmore (1988)

To the left of the main entrance is the window of the old lamp room and beyond this the window of the 'New Chapel', dates from about 1600. This high pointed window, the upper portion of which is 'blind', extends to the level of the first floor rooms. The lower portion of this window can be seen in what is now the 'servants' hall'.

The North Front

21

A STRANGE STORY

This is a story that I used to tell to the scouts at camp around the fire at night.

In 1942, during the War, in December on a cold frosty clear night about 11pm, I was coming home to the Hall down the 'Walk' after being on Home Guard duty in Hunts Cross.

As I approached the Hall there was what appeared to be a light coming from the north entrance. There had been an air raid earlier, so I thought that perhaps an incendiary bomb had fallen and was burning itself out on the bridge. By the time I reached the north lawn entrance I could see that it was not a big light but two small ones coming from the servants' hall and north entrance. I could not understand the reason for these lights, as a black-out was in force and no lights should have been on. It was my duty to inspect and extinguish them.

I rode on to the top of the back bridge and, leaving my bicycle, I walked along the side path towards the north entrance. As I approached the top of the bridge time seemed to stand still. I seemed to be walking in a dream. The light at the entrance was a candle in a lantern, the wicket gate in the main door was open, and a figure in a robe was standing inside. I could see his face. It was a man in his fifties. His hair around his bald patch was grey. It had been dark in his youth for the eyebrows were thick, dark and bushy. The face reminded me of someone but who it was I could not remember at that time.

The figure was a priest who invited me in and led me through the side door on the left. We had entered a chapel. Candles were lit on the altar. I could not manage to tell him that there was a war on and a blackout was in force. Time did not seem to matter. He invited me to kneel at the altar and gave me a blessing. I was then led out to the door, and an alms dish was held out to me. The only change I had in my pocket was a 2/6d coin and I placed it in the alms dish. I was then ushered out of the main entrance and onto the bridge. At the end of the bridge I looked back. The lights had gone out.

Time had returned to the present. I could not find anything wrong so I returned to my bicycle and went into the Hall by the kitchen entrance. In the morning after dressing, I went to collect my change to put it in my pocket. I was 2/6d short. Memory of the night before came back to me. I immediately went to the lamp room at the front entrance. Just inside the door was a tin lid with 2/6d in it.

I recalled the priest and I realised where I had seen him before. His face had been that of the Rev. Canon Edward John Norris who had died in 1937.

***

In the gable-end above the bedroom over the servants' hall and under the finial was an entrance to one of nesting boxes in the roof space. During spring and summer we had owls nesting in this box. We were able to tell if the owls were in occupation by the pellets on the ground under this chapel window.

Going through the wicket gate into the large porch, on the left of the entrance is the lamproom.

Each morning, the oil lamps were collected after the night's use and taken into the lamp room where they were prepared for the next night. The wicks were trimmed, glass funnels cleaned and polished and the oil containers were partly filled with paraffin. They were not filled because if a lamp was left standing for some time in a cool room and then taken into a warm room, the oil would expand, overflow and leak on to the table. Each morning this was the first duty of the odd-job man George Quint.

The cleaning of the glass funnels took much time and care. The inside of the glass funnel was cleaned with a cotton bung on a wire holder. The bung was about one and a half inches in diameter. This was pulled up and down inside the funnel for about five minutes, accompanied by much hot breath on the glass. The same treatment was then given to the outside of the funnel, but this time with a soft cotton cloth.

Wicks were treated with the same respect. They were trimmed with a pair of cutters, to make them parallel. They were then withdrawn into their holder until they were level with the top. The first finger and thumb was used to smooth the top of the wick.

This operation made sure of a level flame and a good light.

This work would take about thirty minutes for each lamp. The number of lamps cleaned depended on the time of year. As he carried out this work Quint always whistled a hymn, very much out of tune and hard to recognise. I have spent many hours watching him doing this work. After the lamps had been overhauled they were placed on a small table outside the housekeeper's room for use during the next night.

On entering the courtyard, one is immediately captivated by the magnificence of the two Irish yew trees, now over 400 years old. They are called Adam and Eve, Eve being the thin one. It is said that the wood from these trees may have provided the bows and arrows used by our ancestors when they fought under the Norris leadership in the Tudor wars with France.

When we lived at the Hall, and for some time afterwards, there was always a tawny owl in one of the yew trees! At night we could hear it hooting and sometimes it would drop down to take a mouse in the courtyard. The hoot of the owl would make the Hall seem very eerie and ghostly, especially at night.

The courtyard is crossed from north to south by a wide pathway paved with 'kidney stones'. Until 1932 each side of this pathway was just earth. I can remember in that year a load of kidney stones being brought in on a horse-drawn cart and tipped on to the centre path. The stones were then laid by the gardeners and outside workers to look just as they do now. However the laying of these stones made it very difficult to brush up the spines from the Yew trees.

Before the north side was built in 1598, the main entrance to the Hall was in the south side of the courtyard. Above the main entrance door on the south side is an eavesdropping hole, and behind the hole is a room where a person could stand and listen to what is being said at the entrance below. It is said that in the 16th century Speke Hall was a safe house for priests and that there would always be priests in the house. If for some reason, they had to hide, there are many hiding places in the house. (The modern term to eavesdrop is to listen to a secret or private conversation.)

'Eavesdropping' Room looking down

Eavesdropping Room

Whip Holder

The north corridor runs from the west side of the entrance. Just inside the door of this corridor at the top of the wall is what appears to be a doorstop. In fact it is a whip holder for carriage whips. It is about six inches in diameter and I can remember two long whips always hanging on this double holder. Under these whips was a blanket chest containing coach rugs. One was made of cat skins.

The wallpaper is a William Morris paper of 1862 in the 'Trellis' design. This paper was re-blocked and replaced after we left the Hall.

In the corridor outside the breakfast room was an ancient chair. This chair was said to be a so-called 'Penance Chair'. It had an assortment of nails (now bent over) in the seat. It was said that these nails protruded through the seat and for penance a person had to balance over them with their arms on the arm-rests. No cushions were provided!

The breakfast room (now in the guide books called the "Small Dining Room") is at the end of the north wing. The east wall contains a robust 'blind' stone chimneystack, which is not self-evident from within and was never a ground floor fireplace. It was constructed as part of a system of secret hiding places allegedly connecting with an escape passage, but, as this passage has been filled in and bricked up for hundreds of years, it can not be said for certain that in fact this passage ever existed.

The Norrises, or any of the other trustees when they stayed at the Hall, had their breakfast served to them each morning in this room and then used it as a sitting room. It always seemed to us a warm and cosy room when we went to see the guests during their visits to the Hall. We were called in to see them on each visit so that they could see how we were progressing. They always gave us some money, usually two shillings and six pence.

The room officially called the "Billiard Room" is at the corner of the north and west corridors and was formerly used as a kitchen. It became a billiard room in the 19th century.

The west corridor always appeared to be dark and dismal, not a pleasant walk on a dark night and it has a very unhappy memory for me.

On the 1st April 1929 my mother died of pneumonia. I was then 6 years old. I asked my relations, who were staying with us at that time, where my father was. They said that he had gone to the billiard room. I set off from our living room to find him.

This walk took me through the screen door of the Great Hall, across the Great Hall past 'Peter' (the suit of armour) standing at the door leading to the west wing and along the corridor to the billiard room. Just inside the door on two trestles was a coffin and in it was my mother. I looked at my mother for the last time and returned to the east wing. My father was not there. I do not remember being frightened or at all disturbed. I cannot even remember telling anyone about it at the time.

*Billiard Room
Entrance*

*The West Corridor
from Billiard Room,
taken 1934*

My brother Frank was at this time in hospital, also with pneumonia. He did not return home to the Hall until June of that year. During the time our father was visiting the hospital to see our mother, the Quint family looked after me.

In 1914 Miss Watt gave the billiard table to the Garston Men's Club. This table was never returned and is now lost. ✳ *since this book was written it has been returned + is awaiting refurbishment*

Next door to the billiard room is the Hall's library. This room was used by Miss Watt as an estate office. During our time at the Hall it was kept locked and only opened for cleaning or if the books had to be consulted. They were of little interest to us, so this did not happen very often.

27

The "Gun Room" was used as an estate office until 1940. In 1932 Sutton Grange was sold off with other parts of the estate to the Liverpool Corporation for the Airport. Previous to this, the guns were kept there. I can remember a .410 shotgun belonging to Miss Lee Steere was there. She also had a single shot .22 rifle for shooting the rooks in the trees of the Clough Wood. In later years I used both these guns to shoot rabbits, rats, and any other vermin that I found within the Hall grounds. During the years before 1939, when the shooting parties visited, they used this room to assemble their 12 bore shotguns and later after the shoot to clean them.

In the north and west corridors there are three glass cases, two of birds and one containing animals. These cases were originally in the north and west galleries. Two of the cases were on a cupboard outside the "Tapestry Room" and the other between the "Blue Bedroom" and the "State Dressing Room".

The one in the west gallery contains a wild cat with a young rabbit in heather. This is now in the north corridor outside the billiard room. I was always told that this had come from the Watt estate at Spott House, Haddingtonshire, Scotland. Of late, some doubt has been cast on the origin of this animal. It has been suggested that it may be a civet from Africa or Asia. I do not believe that Miss Watt would have allowed a foreign animal to be put into a case with Scottish heather and a young rabbit.

Between the library and the billiard room is a case containing a barn owl, cock pheasant, and a tawny owl. The third case at the end of the west corridor by the main staircase, contains a curlew, woodpigeon, sparrow hawk and duck.

The floors of the Great Hall and corridors are of stone. This made them ideal for roller skating and playing marbles.

I cannot remember going into the Great Hall for the first time, for it has always seemed to have been part of my life. Nevertheless, I do remember the tea parties on the big table in the centre of the Hall and the armour being taken down from over the fireplace and put on this table to be cleaned and greased. My brother and I always hoped we would be around when the staff did this.

When the trustees came to visit us they always had their meals on a small table in the south bay with a fire in the open fireplace. My father served these meals from the sideboard, which is on the left of the main entrance. The sideboard panels date from about 1600, and depict a Biblical scene from the Book of Esther (and is now in the Oak Parlour).

West Door and 'Peter'

Another memory I have is of the suit of armour which we called Peter, which stood guard at the west door. Many times I have tried the helmet on. This suit of armour is a 19th century reproduction. I was always impressed by how bright and light the Great Hall was in the daytime and how very dark it was at night, except on a moonlight night when the moon was shining through the windows on the south side. It always felt very cold by the door leading from the screens side under the "Minstrels' Gallery"!

The Great Hall Fireplace

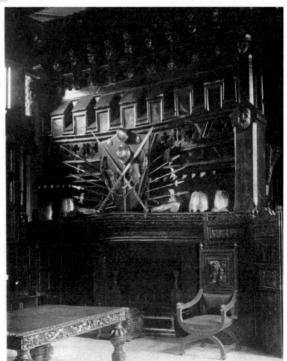

The reason for this chill can perhaps be explained by the ghost story related on page 38. In 1935 when electricity was installed throughout the Hall, a large chandelier was hung in the centre of the Great Hall. It had forty candle positions and had probably been used in the past. At that time it was converted and wired to take candle lamps. At the same time two six-light chandeliers held by arms with the hands were placed on each side of the fireplace. A six-light chandelier lighted each of the bays. The great wainscot on the west wall has always impressed me. For a long time I understood that it had been looted from Holyrood Palace, but

29

this is not so. It is probably Flemish panelling imported by Edward Norris in 1562-3, with its inscription, which reads.

'SLEEPE NOT TELL YE — HATHE CONSEDERD — HOW THOU HATHE — SPENT YE DAYE PAST — IF THOU HAVE WELL DON — THANK GOD — IF OTHER WAYS — REPENT YE'

I have always been able to remember this inscription.

The first telephone installed at the Hall was situated in the screen corridor. To charge the telephone line a handle had to be turned before and after making the call. Later we had a hand set on a table. The telephone number was Garston 131.

To use the telephone we had to come from the housekeeper's room in the servants' quarters. On dark nights this would entail carrying an oil lamp to light the way.

The "Blue Drawing Room" measures some 23ftx16ft. When we moved into the Hall in 1926 we had use of this room as a lounge. It was also used throughout the years as a dining room for the shooting parties. In 1933 the room was redecorated for our use. The paper used was a William Morris paper. It was hung by E .W. Kneen & Sons of Garston. The paper used was found in one of the cupboards in the Hall and I understand that it was a paper bought in 1864 for this room and not used until this time much later.

When we used this room the furniture was part of the suite in Louis XV style. The two rectangular tables and the two kidney shaped tables were part of the furnishings.

Blue Drawing Room

I can remember when we spent Christmas in this room, with a big fire in the fireplace and a Christmas tree in the corner by the window lit with ordinary candles, not electric lamps. It was a very cosy room, being light in the summer and warm in the winter. The room was an ideal size for us to use for our many games, which included boxing.

In the "Oak Drawing Room" or "Great Parlour" there is, on the west side, a bay window with seats built round it. During the summer months I would go and sit in this bay and read or play games. It was always quiet and peaceful.

The main staircase is not very impressive as an example of a main staircase of a big house. On this staircase there stood a very fine pair of old chairs dating from about 1600. They were known as 'wishing chairs'. One was on the half landing, and the other on the first floor landing.

The legend says that a wish must be started in one and completed in the other. I have made many wishes in these chairs, but cannot say whether they have ever come true, because I could never remember the wish after I had made it. I would like to believe that they have.

Wishing Chair

Thunderbox

At the end of each of these landings there is a small room. These contain Victorian water closets. Until about sixty years ago they were in working order. The seats are made of wood and the handle in the seat was pulled to flush the lavatory. There is a box at the side to hold magazines and a wooden hinged cover. When these water closets were advertised in the Victorian papers they were known as 'Thunderboxes'.

31

The "State Bedroom" is a splendidly panelled room, which stands at the northwest corner of the building above the billiard room. It is in this room that King Charles I is reputed to have slept around the year 1630, during one of his visits to Liverpool.

A story I was told as a boy is that during his stay at Speke Hall King Charles I. planted an oak tree on the south lawn. Until about sixty years ago this tree was on the west side of the south lawn.

The stump of the old tree is still visible and is about 6ft in diameter. I can remember climbing on and sitting under this tree. I would like to think that perhaps this story is true. The tree was of a size to have been planted in the 1630s.

From the windows of this room I would shoot rabbits with the .410 shotgun. The rabbits would be feeding on the grass in the filled in moat.

On the door of this bedroom there is an unusual bolt. There is a flat bar on a swivel attached to the inside of the door. This can be turned across the door case. On the door-case is a bolt, which runs in two saddles and can be dropped over the bar. From the pull-cord by the bed a wire runs over pulleys to the bolt, so making it possible for the door to be bolted on the inside and controlled from the bed.

The 'Priest Room'
Hiding Place

32

The "Green Bedroom", or "Priests Room", is the first bedroom in the north gallery going from the west. In this room, in the west wall, is a great chimneystack. Within the window side of this stack is a powder-closet, accessible through a door by the side of the fireplace.

The small panel immediately on the left side of the fireplace gives access to a passage and there is a vertical ladder leading to one of the secret hiding-places of the building. Transversing the stack from south to north is a passage leading into a room about 9ft square.

I was about 16 years old when I first explored this room. My heart was in my mouth, not knowing what I would find, but all I found was dust and cobwebs not the chest of treasure that I had hoped for.

Hiding Room

From this ladder there is access to the roof space. The Rev Edward John Norris, Hon. Canon of Christ Church, Oxford, who was one of the trustees of Speke Hall, came to stay two or three times a year between 1926 and 1932. During his visits he would always use this so called "Green Bedroom".

First thing each morning my father would take him hot water. He carried it in a metal can not unlike a watering can, and from it he filled the porcelain jug ready for Rev Norris's morning wash.

In the adjacent "Green Dressing Room", by the window side of the fireplace, is a powder closet. Above this is the entrance to yet another secret way leading to the roof space. Originally this carefully concealed entrance would have had a connection with the "Tapestry Room" next door. Over this room are the initials of Edward and Mary Norris, who used this suite of rooms. The "Green Bedroom" is also fitted with one of the above-described bolts operated from the bed by a pull cord.

The room officially described as the "Tapestry Room" or "Haunted Room" is situated over the main entrance on the north side. This room was Miss Watt's bedroom. The walls were covered with tapestries, one of which covered the door of a cupboard space at the right hand side of the fireplace. The door had a small catch. This space possibly gave access to the lower stack in the "Small Dining Room" below and thence out of the Hall altogether. The fireplace in this room is one of the few original ones in the house still surviving. It dates from 1595.

For years I have known, from what I can remember of stories told to me by old retainers at Speke Hall, of a staircase situated in the "Tapestry Bedroom" behind the door on the right-hand side of the fireplace, at that time concealed behind the tapestry. This staircase ran from the roof space through the "Tapestry Bedroom" down to the "Small Dining Room" to a space on the left of the dummy fireplace at the east end of this room, (now covered by the organ). From this position I was told that it connected to an underground tunnel and out of the Hall into the moat area.

I remembered reading about this staircase in a book, the title of which I could not remember.

Recently I was given from the archives at Speke an account of Joseph Brereton's tenancy at the Hall from 1840 to 1855. In it is stated that he had a visit in 1853 from Harriet Beecher Stowe, the author of 'Uncle Tom's Cabin'. She also wrote 'Sunny Memories of Foreign Lands' in which appears an article about her visit to Speke Hall. This was the book in which I had read about the staircase!

I have added a copy of that article. I have also added a copy of an article I found in the *History of the County of Lancashire Volume 3(1907)'*

Sunny Memories of Foreign Lands
Volume 1, by Harriet Beecher- Stowe.

Article from the book about Speke Hall, 1853:

"After a drive of seven or eight miles, we alighted in front of Speke Hall. This house is a specimen of the old fortified houses of England, and was once fitted up with a moat and drawbridge, all in approved feudal style. It was built somewhere about the year 1500. The sometime moat was now full of smooth, green grass, and then drawbridge no longer remains.

This was the first really old thing that we had seen since our arrival in England. We came up first to a low, arched, stone door, and knocked with a great old-fashioned knocker; this brought no answer but a treble and bass duet from a couple of dogs inside; so we opened the door, and saw a square court, paved with round stones, and a dark, solitary yew tree in the centre. Here in England, I think, they have vegetable creations made on purpose to go with old, dusky buildings; and this yew tree is one of them. It has altogether a most goblin-like, bewitched air, with its dusky black leaves and ragged branches, throwing themselves straight out with odd twists and angular lines, and might put one in mind of an old raven with some of his feathers pulled out, or a black cat with her hair stroked the wrong way, or any other strange, uncanny thing. Besides this they live almost forever; for when they have grown so old that any respectable tree ought to be thinking of dying, they only take another twist, and so live on another hundred years. I saw some in England seven hundred years old, and they had grown queerer every century. It is a species of evergreen, and its leaf resembles our hemlock, only it is longer. This sprig gives you some idea of its general form. It is always planted about churches and graveyards; a kind of dismal emblem of immortality. This sepulchral old tree and the bass and treble dogs were the only occupants of the court. One of these, a great surly mastiff, barked out of his kennel on one side, and the Other, a little wiry terrier, out of his on the opposite side, and both strained on their chains, as if they would enjoy making even more decided demonstrations if they could.

There was an aged, mossy fountain for holy water by the side of the wall, in which some weeds were growing. A door in the house was soon opened by a decent-looking serving woman, to whom we communicated our desire to see the hall.

We were shown into a large dining hall with a stone floor, wainscoted with carved oak, almost as black as ebony. There were some pious sentences and moral reflections inscribed in old English text, carved over the doors, and like a cornice round the ceiling, which was also of carved oak. Their general drift was, to say that life is short, and to call for watchfulness and prayer. The fireplace of the hall yawned like a great cavern, and nothing else, one would think, than a cartload of western sycamores could have supplied an appropriate fire. A great two-handed sword of some ancestor hung over the fireplace. On taking it down it reached to C----'s shoulder, which, you know, is six feet high.

We went into a sort of sitting room, and looked out through a window, latticed with little diamond panes, upon a garden wildly beautiful. The lattice was all wreathed round with jess amines. The furniture of this room was modern, and it seemed the more unique from its contrast with the old architecture.

We went up stairs to see the chambers, and passed through a long, narrow, black oak corridor, whose slippery boards had the authentic ghostly squeak to them. There was a chamber, hung with old, faded tapestry of Scripture subjects. In this chamber there was behind the tapestry a door, which, being opened, displayed a staircase, that led delightfully off to nobody knows where. The furniture was black oak, carved, in the most elaborate manner, with cherubs' heads and other good and solemn subjects, calculated to produce a ghostly state of mind. And, to crown all, we heard that there was a haunted chamber, which was not to be opened, where a white lady appeared and walked at all approved hours. *(This is now the Tapestry Bedroom; there is a door on the right of the fireplace. Tom Whatmore)*

Now, only think what a foundation for a story is here. If our Hawthorne could conjure up such a thing as the Seven Gables in one of our prosaic country towns, what would he have done if he had lived here? Now he is obliged to get his ghostly images by looking through smoked glass at our square, cold realities; but one such old place as this is a standing romance. Perhaps it may add to the effect to say, that the owner of the house is a bachelor, who lives there very retired, and employs himself much in reading.

The housekeeper, who showed us about, indulged us with a view of the kitchen (now the Billiard Room) whose snowy, sanded floor and resplendent polished copper and tin, were sights for a housekeeper to take away in her heart of hearts. The good woman produced her copy of Uncle Tom, and begged the favour of my autograph, which I gave, thinking it quite a happy thing to be able to do a favour at so cheap a rate."

From *'Townships: Speke', A History of the County of Lancashire: Volume 3* (1907):

"On the first of the house corridors run round the inner sides of the north, east, and south ranges, opening to a series of rooms which, apart from their furniture, have little architectural interest. The roof space is, as usual, plastered and clay-floor, but has one unusual feature, a small room with a fireplace over the servants' hall, which, as has been said, may have been the chapel. There is a staircase to this room. It is worthy of note that the ridge of the roof of the north wing is over the centre of the range of rooms on the upper floor, and note over that of the full width of the range including the corridor, which has separate timbers carrying down the slope of the roof. It is possible that this may imply retention of an older arrangement of the house; but nothing else in the detail gives any support to the idea. The gabled roof of the northeast bay window of the hall is apparently a later addition, as the embattled plate of the hall continues behind it, and there is also the head of an upright timber with part of an applied wooden 'buttress' like those elsewhere in the court."

It has always been said that there was an underground tunnel out of the Hall to enable the priests to escape across the Mersey. This could have been made possible by space on the side of either the east or west end chimneybreast of what is now the "Small Dining Room". There is a small bricked up entrance in the wall on the north side immediately opposite the chimneystack of the "Priest's Room" and "Small Dining Room". Could this be the outlet of the tunnel?

This entrance is now behind a lot of shrubbery against the wall, but it was in plain view in the 1900s and 1930s.

↑

Possible Tunnel Entrance

A cradle, which was thought to be Flemish and dating from 1631 has been placed in the window space, to fit in with the ghost story told about this room. However, before I relate the legend I must go into the history of the Beauclerk Family.

On November 9th 1736, at 36 years of age Lady Mary Norris married Lord Sidney Beauclerk, 5th son of Charles, 1st Duke of St Albans who was the illegitimate son of King Charles II and Nell Gwyn. Sidney was a very handsome and thoroughly unscrupulous man of bad character. His contemporaries nicknamed him as 'Worthless Sidney'.

Tapestry Room

They had only one son, Topham Beauclerk, born in 1739, who succeeded to the Speke estate in 1766. He married Diana, daughter of Charles 3rd Duke of Marlborough, on the 12th March 1768. They had three children, a son Charles George and two daughters. Charles George inherited the estate in 1780 but only retained it for 17 years. In 1795 he sold it to Richard Watt, a merchant of Liverpool.

Speke Hall had, by this time, been allowed to degenerate into a dreadful state of decay and it is from this period that we have the legend of the "Tapestry Room". The story concerns a lady of the Beauclerk family living in the Hall during the period between 1736 and 1795, who, finding her husband facing the probability of bankruptcy and ruin, murdered her child by throwing it from the window of this room into the moat. She then committed suicide in the Great Hall by cutting her throat.

Great Hall ghost

It is said that the spirit of this unhappy lady haunts this room and the Great Hall. I cannot say that I ever saw or heard her, in all the 20 years I was in Speke Hall, but I did hear doors banging, floorboards creaking, bells ringing and windows rattling. All these occurrences can of course be explained away in one way or other, but it was always cold by the screen door of the Great Hall.

We had to walk along the corridors or galleries at night with only an oil lamp to light our way. The shadows seemed to move with us and there was the feeling that perhaps we were not alone. We did not linger! In 1935 after electricity was installed, we were then able to flood the corridors and galleries with light. The shadows then faded away but we still had bells ringing and the other noises to explain.

Bathroom

The bathroom, next door to the "Tapestry Room" was installed in the early 20th century for Miss Watt. It is complete with a large bath, fitted with sizable brass taps, from which hot and cold water gushes in great quantities. The room is long and narrow, with a window at the end overlooking the north lawn. The walls are papered with William Morris paper, which is varnished over. During our time at the Hall, I regularly used this bathroom but only during daylight hours and never after dark because it was next door to the room which was allegedly haunted.

THE 3ᴿᴰ CHAPEL

In Herbert Winstanley's book published in 1919 entitled *Speke Hall* it says the following about the 3rd Chapel.

"To the left of the porch is the only arched window in the building. It lights the room now used as the servants' hall and which is supposed to have been the chapel. I have not been able to find any reference to the chapel at Speke Hall, beyond a licence for an oratory there in 1367, though there are two items in Childwall churchwardens' accounts, which may possibly have some bearing on the point. They are under date 1626 and read as follows:

Spent in going to Speake to see the Communion cupp weighed..........VI d.

Pd. To Edmund Holme which was payd for sayd cupp............III. XIII. VI.

Spent in going to his house twpce about the sayd cupp.................XII d

Further reference was made to the 3rd Chapel in Edward John Norris's book of July 1935, *The Building of Speke Hall.*

The chapel lay at the east end of that side of the quadrangle "Wholly built by Edw: N: Esq: ano 1598" Both before and throughout the Tudor times the family were adherents of the Papal claims and had openly resisted the demands of the reformed Church of England. There is evidence that Sir William, exasperated by a churchwarden of Childwall, fought a duel with that worthy for which, and for his refusal to conform, he was fined £1000, a sum subsequently reduced, which must have been comforting.

It appears that he and his family in this corner of Lancashire made no secret of their preference for the old order of faith and worship.

His son Edward was of the same opinion, and in building the northern wing of the hall, made provision for a chapel to serve his family and their dependants. The pointed window under the east bay still remains, though its framework has been renewed from time to time, but it marks the principal window of that portion of the building, which served for religious purposes. Edward Norris seems to have been a man with ecclesiastical leanings, for on two places in his building he introduced the sign of the Cross cut in the lintels of his doorways. The first, as we have seen, is over the entrance to his suite of apartments. The second is the one cut over the small door on the left hand of the entrance gateway. This door gave admittance to the chapel; to which possibly a second entrance opened on the eastern side, either from the courtyard, or from the outer court near the kitchen. It is clear from the examination of the lower timbers which have been severed, and the second doorway leading from the entrance porch into the present passage to the kitchen is of a late construction, and did not exist at the first; nor would it have served any purpose. The partition wall dividing the servants' hall from the passage way was also non-existent in 1598, and was presumably built at the same time as this doorway was made, viz. when the chapel was given up late in the seventeenth century. Records of the Norris family fix this date somewhere about 1650, at which time, for some reason or other, the family renounced the Papacy, and threw in their lot with the religion of the reformed English Church. The ground floor of the chapel must have then covered the space of the servants' hall, the passageway, and the small room to which Edward's doorway now gives admission, for the present wall between this room and the servants' hall was built in the nineteenth century. Thus the area of the chapel would have sufficed for the accommodation of 40 or 50 persons, with perhaps a small vestry screened off on the left of the entrance door, the altar being in the recess under the Gothic window. There is, however, one puzzle, which at present does not admit of certain solution. It is in connection with the large window, the upper part of which is blind. Was this ever clear? Were the ceiling and floor above constructed at a later date? One inclines to view that this was not so, on the ground chiefly that the squire window which lights the room above is symmetrical with the other windows of Edward's building, and it is difficult to think he would have superimposed a squire window on the apex of his Gothic window.

Externally this is what he actually did, but to have lighted his chapel with a squire window above a pointed window is not likely. More probably he would have carried up his Gothic window some three or four feet higher in the wall. It would appear, therefore, that the main timber in the ceiling, which spans the Chapel, was always there, and supported the floor above, and there was no gallery pew for the family, the elevation being too great to serve any practical purpose. How can we then account for the upper portion of this pointed window being now blind? Mr. C. O. Skilbeck. F. S. A. has made the interesting suggestion that it was not always blind, but threw a light on a slanting ceiling from the apex of the window to the noticeable chamfer on the beam, which spans the chapel. When the chapel was disused and became a servants' hall, the floor of the room above was carried out to the window, for greater convenience, and the upper part became blind.

It is unfortunate that the suggestion here advanced can only be conjectural.

A letter dated 1800 is in the writer's possession which mentions that, some years previously, a small pulpit still stood in a corner of the chapel, but what became of it is not known.

Edward John Norris says that the altar would have been in the bay under the Gothic window, this would have been on the north side. Altars are positioned in churches in the east end. I do not think that this statement would be correct

The servants' hall was originally part of the 'New Chapel', built during the construction of the north side in 1598. It was closed soon after 1650 when the Norris family renounced Catholicism. It was then converted in 1878 into the servants' hall. The window at the end, although arched on the outside, is rectangular

The Chapel's Arched Window

42

on the inside. A possible explanation for this is that the upper arched portion of the window may have always been 'blind' to make the chapel window present a characteristically 'ecclesiastical' appearance, from the outside only.

During my father's time as butler to Miss Watt, the servants' hall was in full use. At meal times he would sit at the head of the table. The table would be fully laid for the meal to be served, complete with linen cloth and napkins. The cook or housekeeper would sit at the bottom end of the table. The other servants sat along each side according to the position they held in the household, and of course the lower servants served the meals to the rest.

The Servants' Hall (1920)

After 1926 the carpets from almost all the rooms in the house were stored in this room. These carpets were stored between layers of newspaper sprinkled with turpentine and rolled up. Each year, during the summer, the carpets were taken out-of-doors into the back courtyard, into the sunshine, brushed, and replaced in the servants' hall.

When the room-bells were introduced in the 19th century, the control wires were installed through the roof space or down the corridors. Each room had a bell, controlled by a pull connected to its own bell positioned in three locations. One set was situated at the top of the servants' staircase, another set outside the

Bells outside the Servants' Hall

43

housekeeper's room in the south wing and the third set over the door of the servants' hall in the north wing.

When I lived in the Hall it was not uncommon to hear a bell ring. Generally it was the front door bell but at times one of the others bells would ring. On investigating we would find one of the bedroom bells swinging. As the bedrooms were empty we had no need to answer the call. Our father explained this phenomenon to us. In the roof space lived a selection of livestock including birds, rats, mice, and bats and it would have only required the weight of one of these animals on the wires to set the bells ringing.

At the end of this block is the dairy. Until 1950 it was still equipped as a dairy. The workbenches were slate-topped and milk containers, a butter churn, measuring jugs, butter pads and other equipment were on the shelves. I cannot remember it ever being in use.

On shooting days a wooden rack was erected, and the game shot was hung on it for about a week until it was sold off to the local traders.

My first memory of the kitchen dates back to about 1923-4. It was then that my father took me into Hall to see the staff. I can remember the cook, (who gave me a scone to eat), and all the kitchen staff busily at work.

Kitchen (c.1914)

This room has probably been in use as a kitchen since the time of Sir William Norris. It was added to, and completed by the Watt family. The east wall contains the massive chimneystack. The windows in the bay, which overlook the outer yard, might have formed part of the pre-1300 sandstone building which was part of the early 'Manor of Speke'.

In the 1914 period a new range was installed for Miss Watt. This took the place of the old sunken range. When our family moved into the Hall in 1926 this was the only means of cooking available. As my mother had been a cook in one of the large houses in Herefordshire this range held no terrors for her. In 1928 a more modern range was installed in the butler's pantry.

The Range (1926)

To me the most interesting item in the kitchen is the large table. This has a modern top on the legs of an old table. It is the right size and height for table tennis and this is what we used it for. A look under the tabletop provides proof of this. At the centre at each side can be seen the marks of the net clamps. This room was our games room.

Kitchen table

Kitchen table with tennis net

45

Next door to the kitchen is the scullery. The scullery-maids used to wash up the pots, pans and dishes after the meals. The dishes were put to dry on a wooden rack. This rack stood adjacent to the sink and was still in position when we lived at the Hall.

Scullery (1940)

We used this room as a clothes washhouse. We used the big mangle, which is now in this room. I can remember turning the handle during washing days. The hot water for the house was heated from the stove in this room. It was coke burning and was kept lit day and night. George Quint came in at 7am each morning and 10pm each evening to stoke the fire. Here we cleaned, repaired and kept our bicycles.

As you come in through the back door by the scullery, directly opposite is the vegetable larder. It is a room about 7ftx5ft with a stone bench on each side. Each morning one of the gardeners would bring a selection of vegetables from the kitchen garden to the backdoor. This was a relic from the days of large households and as the vegetable garden was still being worked and we lived in the house, the produce came to us. This morning routine continued until my father left the Hall. Amongst my father's papers was a letter from the Liverpool Corporation agreeing to the continuance of this arrangement. Flowers and vegetables were also sent to Speke Church as required.

The game larder is situated to the left of the butler's pantry and under the menservants' bedrooms. This room is about 20ftx10ft with a rail running down the centre on which the game was hung. Around the walls were stone slab benches. These were for food storage, in cool conditions. We used this room as a general larder and to hang pheasant, hare and rabbit on the rail from time to time.

Miss Watt installed two bathrooms for the servants; one for the men on the ground floor and one for the women above, each had flush toilets alongside. Our family used the one on the first floor during our stay in the Hall. I used the ground floor one as a darkroom for my photography.

The butler's pantry was where the butler cleaned the silver etc. There is a large narrow safe in the wall on the left and a small one under the windows. These were used to store the silver. There are cupboards from floor to ceiling on the right-hand wall, to store the china and glass, and under the sink to store the cleaning materials. In the centre of the room stands a large table. The large sink under the window was made of copper. In the sink there was an oval wooden bowl with zinc bands round it. The idea behind this was to prevent the china and glass from chipping if knocked. A little water was always kept in it to keep it watertight.

Butlers Pantry (1940)

In about 1928 a small coal range was installed in this room for our use and from then we used the butler's pantry as a kitchen. After this range had been in use for about 4 years, a hot spot was found on the wall of the chimneybreast, which ran through the flue of the bedroom above. My father found this hot spot at about 8 o'clock in the evening. There was also a strong smell of burning.

The fire brigade was called at once. They found that an oak beam in the housekeeper's bedroom over the butler's pantry was completely burned through. If this hot spot had not been found, Speke Hall could have been destroyed by fire. I can still recall the smell of burning wood.

Copy of a newspaper cutting in the *Liverpool Daily Post* published between 1932 & 1933:

SPEKE HALL FIRE, TIMELY DISCOVERY SAVES HISTORIC MANSION

The historic Speke Hall, Speke, Nr Liverpool, had a narrow escape from destruction by fire last night when one of the old oak beams in the south wing was discovered to be smoldering by Mr. Whatmore, the caretaker, who lives in the Hall. He noticed a strong smell of burning shortly before ten o'clock and promptly phoned the brigade. The engine from Garston was soon on the scene, followed by the Liverpool Salvage Corps and additional assistance from the central fire station, deputy-chief Superintendent Owen being in charge. The brigade discovered that the beam in the bedroom on the first floor was completely burned through, and soon had the outbreak under control. A quantity of brickwork was removed before the beam could be cut away.

The cause of the outbreak is believed to be due to a defective hearth in the bedroom. The Hall contains many treasures of historic value.

In 1989 during the restoration of the east side, a pair of cruck blades was found in the menservants' bedrooms. These cruck blades are said to date back to the 13th century. It is possible that the beam that had burned through in the 1930s was part of a 13th century building.

It was not until 1935, after electricity had been brought to the hall that we had an electric cooker installed in the butler's pantry.

In 1935 electrical lighting and 5amp sockets were installed thoughout the house, which made it much easier for us to get around the house and of course was much safer from fire risk.

At this time we had an electric cooker installed in the butler's pantry. It was fitted behind the door. The mark of the switch position for this can still be seen on the wall. This room then became our kitchen. We also had a Eureka electric vacuum cleaner, electric iron and kettle. We also had a "Cossor" electric radio.

The Great Hall with Chandeliers

48

There were standard lamps and table lamps fitted throughout the house.

When the house was wired in 1935 there were five chandeliers in the Great Hall wired up for electric lights. They consisted of one three-tier multi light fitting which hung from the centre of the Great Hall, one small one tier fitting in each of the bays north and south, and one on each side of the main fire-place supported out as if held by an arm and hand. At night when these were switched on the Great Hall was completely illuminated.

The dairy alongside the dovecote ran the electrical supply from a supply position at the "North Lodge" in armoured cable down the "Walk" to a sub-station installed in a building. This was a 6000-volt supply and transformed down to 440 volt in this sub-station. When this transformer was supplied it was left out in the rain for a short time and got wet, which was not good for the transformer and it had to be dried out on the range in the kitchen, which took some time.

From this sub-station a supply was taken into the house to a switchboard in a cupboard in the corridor of the servants' hall, this switchboard is still in the cupboard in this corridor.

The electrical installation from this switchboard was carried out in steel conduit and wired in 3.029 V. I. R. cables (Vulcanised Indiana Rubber) throughout the house. A lot of the installation was carried out on the surface. Some of the room lighting switches are still in use. I spent a lot of my time during the school holidays watching and helping (or getting in the way!) Whether this insight into the electrical workings started me off, I do not know, but I ended up being involved in the electrical engineering and contracting industry for all my working life.

Hunters Electrical Contractors of Liverpool carried out this installation. The foreman was a Mr. Jump.

This installation was still in use in the 1950s. It has been rewired a few times up to date (2008.)

During the late 1920s George Quint built crystal sets. One of these was made for our use. A 100ft aerial of copper was put up outside and a wire brought in through the window frame of the butler's pantry with a connection rod, which had a nut at each end for the wire connection. This wire was connected to the crystal set. A 'cat's-whisker' was needed to tune the station in. This was a fine-coiled wire pushed onto the crystal. Getting the right spot on the crystal was a hit and miss affair. When, at last, we did get on to the spot, and the station, my brother and I would listen in on headphones with one earpiece each. The station was a local one, 2LO. The programmes we tried to tune in were "Children's Hour" (with Aunties

Muriel (Levy) and Doris (Campbell)) 'Out with Romany', 'Tales of Toytown with Larry the Lamb' and a programme featuring Derek McCulloch, (Uncle Mac.) His nightly blessing was: - *"Goodnight children, everywhere"*. We progressed in the early 1930's to a valve set, again made by George Quint.

This was a box with two valves on the top, a tuning condenser on the front, and a fixed and movable coil on the side. We had a loudspeaker in the housekeeper's room. This was a 6-inch speaker on a large baffle board. Dry and wet batteries powered this set. The wet battery, called an accumulator had to be charged up every 7 days.

This had to be done in a shop in Garston and it was my job to take the spare battery to be charged. I can remember spilling the acid on my coat causing holes to appearing a week later. By 1934 we had a commercially made set, still powered with batteries.

Back Staircase

By the housekeeper's room is the back staircase leading to the nursery, the "Minstrels Gallery", and all the servants' bedrooms. At the bottom of this staircase buckets of coal were kept for our use in the housekeeper's room. We were grateful for this strong staircase during the 1939-45 War (more about this in the chapter on 'Speke Hall in Wartime').

At the bottom of the stairs was an area screened off for the cleaning of the household's boots and shoes. There was a knife-cleaning machine in this room. The houseman did the cleaning when the Watts lived in the Hall. I used this room as a workshop and for carrying out experiments. The fretsaw that had belonged to Miss Lee Steere was kept in this room for our use.

By the side of this room and outside the housekeeper's room, was a butler's tray mounted on two trestles. The oil lamps were stored here, after they had been cleaned and filled ready for the night's use.

The housekeeper's room is at the end of the entrance passage overlooking the courtyard. This room was used by our family as a living room. I can recall the times when we would let our dog, a terrier bitch called Peggy, out through the window of this room into the courtyard for exercise. Sometimes she would kill rats while she was out there. In the centre of the room was a large mahogany table, which could be extended. This table is now in the "Small Dining Room."

There was a mahogany sideboard on the left-hand side, and a three or four seater settee under the window on the courtyard side. On each side of the fireplace was an easy chair. On the fire we would burn both coal and logs. Sometimes we would toast kippers on a long fork in front of this fire for tea. The lighting was by oil lamps and I can remember how dark it was going out into the passage to get to other parts of the house.

Our sleeping quarters were in the servants' bedrooms, and were those of the housekeeper, cook, and maids. They were situated in the east wing. The corridor overlooks the courtyard. The head housemaid had used my room and its window overlooked the back yard. I slept in this room from 1926 to 1946. In the clothes cupboard of this room in 1934 I fitted a rail for my clothes. This rail is made from a cricket wicket. The room is now the kitchen in the administrator's flat and the rail is still in the cupboard (in 2008!)

T. W. Whatmore's Bedroom

Clothes Rail, and Cricket Wicket

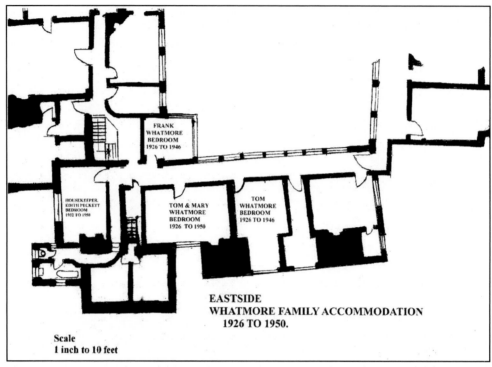

FRANK WHATMORE BEDROOM 1926 TO 1946

HOUSEKEEPER. EDITH PECKETT BEDROOM 1932 TO 1950

TOM & MARY WHATMORE BEDROOM 1926 TO 1950

TOM WHATMORE BEDROOM 1926 TO 1946

EASTSIDE
WHATMORE FAMILY ACCOMMODATION
1926 TO 1950.

Scale
1 inch to 10 feet

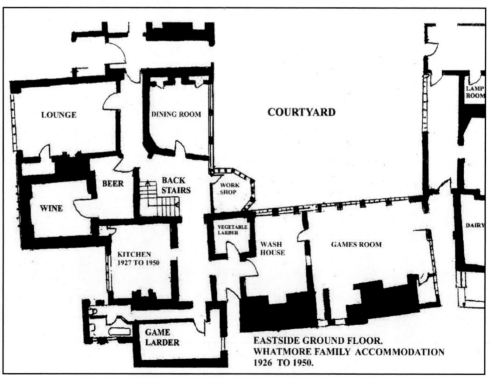

LOUNGE

DINING ROOM

COURTYARD

LAMP ROOM

BEER

BACK STAIRS

WORK SHOP

WINE

VEGETABLE LARDER

DAIRY

KITCHEN
1927 TO 1950

WASH HOUSE

GAMES ROOM

GAME LARDER

EASTSIDE GROUND FLOOR.
WHATMORE FAMILY ACCOMMODATION
1926 TO 1950.

I cannot remember my first visit to the roof space. It was a place to go and explore, but only during the daylight hours. The way in was via a ladder and trap door situated by the nursery in the south wing, or by the 1560 stairway off the west corridor leading to "St Raymond's Room." Our usual way up was by the ladder and trap door.

The only light available was natural light, coming through windows in the gable ends. Using the above mentioned means of entry we had to pass over the Great Hall. The Norris family for sleeping accommodation between 1490 and 1560, had used this space, and after the west side had been completed, it became the servants' quarters. The roof space continues on to the west and north sides.

16th Century Staircase

There was originally a 16th century staircase approached through a low doorway on the west side, immediately opposite the entrance to the Great Hall. The steps wound round a square newel of upright posts. After 1560 when the west side had been completed, the lower section of this staircase was demolished.

In the north wing, positioned in each of the gable ends, were bird-nesting boxes. The entrance to each box was via a small hole under the finials at each of the apexes. These boxes measured about 20"x18"x18", and had sliding doors enabling us to inspect the contents. The birds that came to nest were kestrels, owls and jackdaws. We would always know when the owls were nesting by the pellet droppings on the ground below. It was of great interest to us to see the eggs and then the young birds when we looked through the inspection doors. I had at different times a kestrel, and, at another time, two jackdaws. I kept these birds in the washhouse and, after a period of about a year, let them go into the woods. The young birds I reared were fed on raw liver from the butchers for which I paid a penny or tuppence.

In the roof space over the main entrance in the north wing is a fireplace, now bricked up. Servants or soldiers could have used this in the 17th century. Alongside this fireplace is an area that is said to have been used as a cock-fighting pit.

Roof Space over the West Wing (1935)

Roof Space North side

The priest's exit from the bedroom referred to as the "Green Bedroom" or "Priest's Room" comes out in the roof space. Alongside the chimney stack of this room is the priest's hiding hole. It also has an exit here. Next door in the "Green Dressing Room," at the side of the chimneystack, is another way into the roof space.

As one approaches the Hall over the back bridge, the yard in front is covered in cobble or kidney stones. Towards the Hall and under the stones is a water tank, the top covered with a stone slab. The pump situated by the scullery door would have pumped water from this tank. It is said that the water supply came from the 'Top Dam' via the sluice gate and filter beds. This supply was changed when mains water was installed in about 1895.

During the War, in 1940, this tank was filled with water by the Fire Service, as a static water supply in case of fire at the Hall. The window of my bedroom, looked out over this yard towards Home Farm.

To the right of the yard at the bottom of the bridge was a coal store. It was here that we had at least a ton of coal delivered at a time. The odd job man brought a daily supply of coal into the House.

Behind the coal place was the paraffin store; in its early days this had been a dovecote.

The washhouse was situated to the left of the yard and extended out from the game-larder with a passage between. Entrance was gained from this passage on the left. Directly opposite the door on the far wall there were two large copper boilers built up on bricks over a fire hole.

On the front wall under the windows stood six large earthenware sinks. In the centre was a coal burning stove with a round flue pipe going up through the roof. This stove was used for heating the ironing irons. The washhouse was complete with a very large mangle.

When we first moved into the Hall all our washing was done here but eventually our washing was done in the scullery. We then used the sinks in the washhouse as tanks to keep all sorts of pond life, such as the larva of the cadis and dragon fly, water-beetle, water-boatman and any other water specimens we acquired.

To get these specimens we would drag the streams and ponds with a jam-jar on a string. To catch small fish we would set a jam-jar in the stream against the run of the water, so that the small fish would swim in and be caught.

When I was about 14 years old I had two tame jackdaws. I kept them flying loose in the washhouse. To feed them I would only have to call "Jack!" and they would come and sit on my shoulder to be fed daily on raw liver. After about a year I let them go into the back yard, they stayed around for about another 6 months before going off into the woods.

The back of the laundry was used as an ironing room. It had a long bench under the window on the south side. In the centre of the room was a table for ironing the sheets; the irons would be heated on the stove in the washhouse.

During 1934, the buckled windows throughout the Hall were being repaired and releaded. The workers carried out this work on the bench in the ironing room. The process was firstly to take out the window from the wooden frame, and then it was laid out on the tabletop. All the old lead was stripped off the glass and the pieces of glass laid out in order. Next the strip of new lead was passed through an extruder to stretch it into the 'H' section of correct size. It was then cut into pieces to suit the glass size and placed around the glass. Resin powder was placed on each joint as a flux.

Two soldering irons were placed on top of the stove in the washhouse to get hot. The use of one iron at a time enabling the glazier to have a continual hot iron, which was placed on each joint. The solder spread like a bubble of water over each joint. When all the joints were soldered and the window completed, the new window was fixed back into its wooden frame. I spent many hours watching and learning.

Back Courtyard (1935)

This washhouse had been installed for Miss Watt during the late 1800s or early 1900s.

The dry lavatories and a midden were placed at the end of the washhouse, outside, away from the Hall. The midden had a way in at the rear, so that it could be cleaned out. A man entered with a spade and emptied it into a horse drawn cart placed at the front. The midden and lavatories had to be emptied about four times a year. This was done until the Hall was taken over by the Liverpool Corporation in 1943.

At the east side of the yard, over the boiler house, was the dog kennel and next door to this a storeroom. Peggy, our small white terrier, was kept there during the day, tethered on a long chain so she had the run of the yard. At night she was brought into the house. She was an extremely good guard dog and lived to be 15 years of age.

It was in this storeroom that we found Miss Watt's invalid chair, which my brother and I used as a chariot. The new toilets are now built on this site.

Washhouse (1970)

Under these buildings is the central heating boiler house. To get to it there was a set of stone steps alongside the dog kennel. At the top of these steps was a hole with a cast iron cover. It was through this hole that the coke for firing the boilers was tipped.

Inside the boiler house were two boilers. These had to be continually stoked with coke to keep the Hall at a reasonable temperature. It was one of the jobs performed by George Quint. He would bank up the fire every night at 10pm

57

and again in the morning at 7am. Each day the fires required cleaning out. They would be raked, the clinker taken out and disposed of outside in the area of the old moat. I have helped to do this many times

The central heating system was installed for Miss Watt during 1895. It consists of 4 to 5 inch cast iron piping running throughout the house, with radiators in most rooms. It was a gravity-fed system and was most efficient. When the system got too hot, the piping would rattle and bang making a terrible noise. This central heating system is still in use. The only modification, as far as I know, has been the installation of oil-fired boilers.

To the left of the boiler house was a storeroom and workshop. It had a workbench under the window, complete with a joiner's vice. It was in here that I did a lot of my joinery, under instruction from George Quint.

HOUSEKEEPERS 1929-1950

The first housekeeper in this period was a Mrs. Whitfield. She came to the Hall just after our mother's death and stayed for about a year. She was a very kind person but for some reason she could not stay with us.

In early May 1930 Mrs. Christine Miller Barr Hitchmough came as housekeeper. I remember her coming quite well. It was just before my 8th birthday and she gave me a birthday card. The reason why I remember this card is that it had a cat on it, which, when it was pressed made a sound. She stayed for about a year and had to leave for family reasons. It is a strange coincidence that this lady was the great aunt of my future wife.

Mrs. Edith Peckett,
Housekeeper (1932-1950)

Mrs. Christine Miller Barr Hitchmough,
Housekeeper (1930)

I did not think I would ever see her again. In 1945 I became engaged to a Miss Peggy Atkin. I was taken to see her aunt, her mother's sister. The grandmother in the house was a Mrs. Hitchmough, the lady that had been our housekeeper in 1930. Yet another strange coincidence!

Peggy and I married in 1946 and in the late 1970s the house next door to us was for sale. The family that moved in was the Hitchmough Family, which included Jim Hitchmough (the Liverpool playwright and author) who was the grandson of Mrs. Hitchmough and a cousin to my wife.

During the years 1930 to 1932 we had a number of housekeepers. None of these ladies stayed very long. They did not give any reasons for leaving. One of these ladies had a five-year-old daughter. At night she would string cotton across the door to her bedroom. It was never disturbed and was always intact in the morning! However, she did not stay.

Another lady during this period came one evening to collect me from school. She asked me if I would go home with her. I said that I wanted to go home to the Hall. I was given a note and sent off on my own. On arriving at the Hall I gave the note to my father. It would appear that the lady did not want to return. The next day she sent for her bags. When I told my father that she had wanted me to go home with her he was quite disturbed. I was asked quite a lot of questions but nothing came of it.

All these ladies slept in what we called the housekeeper's room, but the listed name was the "Ladies Maid's Room". This room is in the oldest part of the house and perhaps, with only oil lamps to light the room, the ladies who used the room were afraid of the shadows.

In 1932 Mrs. Edith Peckett came to us as housekeeper. We never did find out her age, but she must have been about forty at that time. She was a widow. Her husband had been the manager of the Alhambra Theatre. Bradford. On her day off each week (Thursday) she would go to the hairdresser and then see her sister, returning to the Hall about 9 o'clock. Her hair was ginger and she kept it that colour all the time we knew her.

She was not a person you could get close to, but was kind and a great help to us. She was a woman of strong character and very dignified. She stayed at the Hall until my father retired in 1950.

The housekeeper's room, or "Ladies Maid's Room," was situated at the south end of the servants' corridor on the east side. It was always said that this section of the Hall was part of the 14th century building. In 1989 the east side was being renovated and in the footmen's rooms, behind some Victorian panelling, the builders found a set of cruck blades and tie beams from medieval times.

The room was about 10ft wide and 18ft long, with a fireplace in the east wall and a 6ft long window in the south wall. The room was furnished with a Victorian brass and iron single bed set against the north wall facing the window, a dressing table under the window, and a washstand, complete with jug and bowl, to the right. Just inside the door on the west wall was a large chest-of-drawers. During the day, as it faced the south, it was bright and light but at night it was rather dark.

In 1932 Mrs. Edith Peckett came to take care of us. She was a woman of strong character indeed! It was not until 1935 that she told us about the visions she thought she had experienced during some nights. She put these visions down to dreams or nightmares, but one night in 1935, in the early hours, she suddenly woke up to find what appeared to be a figure standing by the bed and bending over her. The figure, she said, was dressed in black. She could not see the face. When she sat up the figure disappeared. She was so disturbed by this that she told us all about it the next morning and could not attribute it to a dream or nightmare.

However, the figure did not appear again and by the end of 1935 we had electricity installed in the Hall so the rooms could be flooded with light.

Mrs. Peckett the housekeeper slept in this room. From that night in 1935 she did not see or hear anything else of a spooky nature. Is it possible that the early housekeeper's in 1929-32 saw something and did not like to say (but found it easier to leave?).

Connected with the 'apparition' story of Mrs. Peckett I would like to narrate the following. In October 1934 I had an attack of tonsillitis, and was confined to my bed. I was then 12 years old. My bedroom was off the servants' corridor, in the east wing. It had been the head housemaid's room during the time the Hall was occupied by Miss Watt. It was over the kitchen, one of the oldest parts of the Hall.

I was confined to my bed for 7 days and on about the 3rd day, at about 9 o'clock in the evening, I suddenly woke up to find someone standing by the side of the bed. It was a shadowy figure dressed in black. I could not make out any shape. I sat up and the figure disappeared. It was dark and I could not light the oil lamp, as I was not allowed to have any matches.

I got out of bed and walked along the corridor to the top of the back staircase. I do not remember doing this but I do remember being off the bottom of the staircase where an oil lamp was burning outside the housekeeper's room. I also remember going into the room. After a short time I was taken back to bed. An oil lamp was left burning for me.

Whether this was the result of my illness and the dark room, or whether I did really see someone there, I do not know. I did not repeat the experience of seeing someone, although the feeling of not being alone was constant. This was however not a frightening feeling.

STAFF STORY FROM 1923-1926

My father told me in the 1950s, and by Mrs. Quint about the same time, and later by the kitchen maid, Miss Alice Roberts, in 1989 about a baby that was born to a young maid in the 1921-1926 period in the Hall.

This baby is said to have been born in the maid's room and hidden in a suitcase. A report of this scandal was in the local paper of that time. I understand from people that have lived in the house over the last few years that a baby's cry has been heard in these rooms, but none of my family ever heard the cries.

The Liver Sketching Club South Front (1931)

CHAPTER 3

OUT AND ABOUT

As the Hall was our home, so the grounds and woods were our playground. As therefore, with the house, the grounds also hold many memories for me. On a walk round I will try to point out places of interest.

We start our walk by going out of the Hall by the south entrance. This was built by Edward Norris in 1605 and bears the initials E. N. and M. N. It was in the vicinity of this entrance that all the family photographs were taken during the 20 years we lived in the Hall. The view from this entrance was magnificent looking towards the river through the Clough, or Blue Bell Wood. Over the years it was from here that we always started our walks in the grounds.

In the 1930s each year we had a visit from the Liver Sketching Club. The man in the archway, the president of the Club in 1931, is Mr. Albert Kneen of Garston. In 2006, 75 years later, the Club recreated the same scene. I would then have been 9 years old when the picture to the left was taken. I attended the visit of the Club to Speke Hall on Tuesday July 25th 2006 when the modern day artists recreated this magical scene from 75 years ago.

The Liver Sketching Club (2006)

In the 1920s and early 1930s, a horse-drawn mower cut the south lawn. The carthorse was brought down from the Home Farm and it would have taken two men a full day to cut the grass. One would walk behind the mower while the other led the horse.

In about 1932 a motor mower was purchased, requiring only one man's labour. It still took a full day to cut the grass.

The Ha-Ha

At the top end of the lawn is a ha-ha, which gave the impression that the lawn continued on to the farm field, and that the animals could just walk onto the lawn. There was, until about 1975, a great oak tree growing in the left hand side of the lawn. The gardeners told me that King Charles I during his visit to the Hall had planted it in the 1630s. There is no written record of this. The tree has now been cut down, but the stump can still be seen.

South Lawn and Oak Tree

Our walk continues along the top of the ha-ha and down the south side. As we get half way down, looking across to the north side you can see, through the entrance, the 'Walk'. From this point in the centre of the lawn we could keep a lookout for anyone coming to the Hall. It was here that we had our cricket pitch where we played most summer evenings with our friends. Progressing along the south side, we come to what was the entrance to the Bluebell Wood. As one looks back at the Hall from this point, the new finial on the top of the gable end over the nursery can be seen. Eli Warren (the carpenter in 1932) made this.

THE CLOUGH WOOD, OR BLUE-BELL WOOD

Picture a 12ft wide path through an avenue of trees. In spring the new green leaves meet at the tops of the trees. Each side of the path is blue and yellow; blue with the colour of bluebells and yellow with primroses. It was such a picturesque sight that people came from all over the country to see and paint it. The Liver Sketching Club was one of the groups of artists that came to draw and paint this wood and the Hall.

During the spring and summer evenings we would, sometimes, walk through the wood to the Mersey shore. We would go through the gates at the bottom of the path and walk along the cliff top without meeting a single person. In the late evening we would return through the woods enjoying the smell of the bluebells and the sound of birds. We would see the pigeons, rooks, owls and many other birds coming in to roost in the Clough Wood.

It was possible to see, running through the undergrowth, field mice, rabbits, stoats, weasels and an occasional cat that had become wild. If you were quick you could catch a small rabbit under the Rhododendron bushes.

During the early part of World War II, in 1942, this wood was cut down to allow the aircraft to land in safety at Liverpool Airport. After this the wood did not seem the same. The birds and wild life could not use the trees as shelter and went to other parts of the estate. In later years, when the new runway was cut through the bottom part of the Clough, a high bank was built to shelter the Hall from the vibrations from the taxiing aeroplanes.

Returning from the Clough Wood we arrive at the top of the moat, now drained and grassed over. It is said that the draining was done during the 17th century. During our early years at the Hall this area served us as a football field and a place to practise riding our bicycles up and down the banks. The moat continues around the Hall to the north side.

Clough Wood by Tom Whatmore (1989)

The Liver Sketching Club North Front (1933)

The North Front by Mr. J. Walton Burnett (1933), called Autumn Tints

It is said that the exit from the secret passage came out on the north side. The Liver Sketching Club made drawings and paintings of this side of the Hall too. One of the artists, a Mr J Walton Burnett, painted in 1933, a water colour and called it 'Autumn Tints'. We enjoyed playing in the Clough Wood, and once we built a small log cabin, just off the moat on the west side.

67

With the north lawn in front of us, we take the road to the left, through the top end of the Clough Wood and over what was (until 1849) the "Lower Dam". At the end of this road was the "West Lodge" which was built for Miss Watt to accommodate one of the workers on the estate. For a short time between 1923 and 1925, we lived in this lodge before our move into the Hall. The accommodation in the lodge consisted of a living room with coal range, two small bedrooms, and a scullery with a stone sink with cold water only. It was demolished after my father left the Hall.

Standing with our backs to where the "West Lodge" stood and facing away from the Hall, in front of us is Banks Lane, the Molynoux Meadow to the left, and Great Plumb Field to the right. Banks Lane ran from Speke Hall past Sutton Grange on the left to the Chapel House Farm and then on to Banks Road, Garston. This was a lane about 10ft wide with a hawthorn hedge on each side. The distance from the Hall to Garston was about a mile. Sutton Grange was the estate house and office.

Richard Ashby Graves was the estate agent at Speke Hall for Adelaide Watt. In the 1891 Census records he was listed as living at Sutton Grange, Banks Lane, Speke Hall, Speke. He lived there with his family which, in 1891 consisted of his wife Elizabeth, three sons, and three daughters.

Richard was born in Norwood, Norfolk. In the 1891 Census he is listed as being 47 years old. He was still the Agent at the Hall in 1926 when Speke Hall and the estate were closed down. He would then have been about 72 years old.

It is said that he was an impressive man and used to ride round the estate on horseback. It is said that the car he owned was a Buick.

Sutton Grange was a very big estate house complete with stables, coach house, and outhouses for servants. It was situated midway between the West Lodge and Chapel House Farm on Banks Lane. Banks Lane ran between the Walk, passing the Dam to Banks Road, Garston.

I can remember going to Sutton Grange in about 1926 to a November fireworks party with the Graves family before they left.

I visited Sutton Grange many times during the years between 1926 and 1932, to explore the outbuildings and play in the grounds with Fred and Ron Lucas who lived in one of the servants' houses with their parents. I can remember looking into one of the buildings and seeing a coach. What happened to it I do not know. I can remember a time when the farmer had his ram enclosed in the small paddock, and we would try to ride on its back. He was a great sturdy beast. We never did get to ride him, but trying was a lot of fun for us (but not for the ram!)

Sutton Grange was used by the trustees, as an estate office until it was demolished in the1930s The estate secretary was a Mrs. Ellen May Fowler, who was the youngest daughter of Richard Ashby Graves and had become estate secretary to Adelaide Watt before the latter's death in 1921.

The house was situated about 400 yards from the West Lodge. In about 1931 the hay in the barn caught fire. The heat in the centre of the stack caused slow combustion. The fire brigade was called but the pressure of water was so low that it only came out of the hose in a trickle. Unfortunately the barn burned down, much to the delight of all the local children and to the despair of the farmer.

Sutton Grange

WILLIAM BAILEY (BILL), Chauffeur. Born on the 8th March 1882 in a village near Birmingham by the name of Little-Astone. His mother died when he was a baby and his grandmother then brought him up. In his early teens he went into service with the McCorkindale family and then with the Dunlifth family. With these families he rose to the position of footman. It was during this time that he saw his first motorcar and decided that he would like to become a chauffeur. He paid £100 to the Hyde Park Motor Company to be taught all about the motorcar of that time. Before the First World War he applied for the post of chauffeur at Speke Hall to drive for Mrs. Starkie, Miss Watt's aunt. Mrs. Starkie interviewed him for this position at the Adelphi Hotel in Liverpool. He was successful in gaining the position of chauffeur to Mrs. Starkie. The car he drove was an Armstrong Siddley. On the 4th March 1913 he married Mary Agnes White, daughter of Moses White who was gamekeeper at Speke Hall. Bill and his wife went to live at 67 Speke Road Garston. They had twin sons, Frank and Alfred, born on the 23rd December 1913. When the First World War started in June 1914 he volunteered and left Speke Hall for the duration of the war. During this time Mrs. Starkie had the car stored away in Sutton Grange. On his return he took up his position as chauffeur as before.

When Mrs. Starkie died in 1925 he always said that he brought his lady back from the crematorium in a little urn. In her will she left him £600. This news appeared in the *Liverpool Echo* as *'Speke Chauffeur Left £600'*. Two other cars were at the Hall at this time, a Daimler belonging to Miss Watt and a Buick belonging to the estate agent. The three cars were garaged at Sutton Grange. Agnes died on the 13th June 1934 aged 55 years and Bill on the 17th February 1969 aged 87. Agnes is buried at Speke Church.

Bill Bailey with the Armstrong Siddley

Returning from Sutton Grange past the West Lodge along Banks Lane towards the Walk we come to Speke Hall's dam.

This top dam is situated in Great Plumb Field and is said to have provided the water supply for the Hall before mains-water was installed. On the Banks Lane side of the dam there is still evidence of a sluice gate and two filter tanks.

Sluice Gate and Filter Tanks

The dam was one of our favourite places. We would walk around it looking at the wild life that abounded within and upon its waters. There were eels, sticklebacks, moorhens, wild duck, kingfishers, water rats and other fresh water life. We did endeavour to fish from time to time, usually without success but we sometimes caught eels.

This was done by casting a line out across the dam and leaving it out all night, with bait on a number of hooks. Next morning, if we were lucky, we would have caught an eel. In all my time at the Hall I did not see anyone catch a fish.

Quite often my brother and I would take our model boats to sail them on the water. Sometimes they got stuck in the middle and we would then have to throw stones to cause a ripple on the water to drive them to the shore. This was not always successful and sometimes, the boat went to the bottom.

The Speke Dam

At the end of the dam was a small pond, which abounded with roach. My earliest recollection of this pond was, watching men fishing one evening and falling into the water. The next thing I knew was finding myself in bed in the Hall. I would then have been about 8 years old. In later years I spent quite a lot of time fishing in this water and caught a lot of fish.

From the dam we walk to the end of Banks Lane along a sunken road built as a ha- ha. This part of Banks Lane was made this way so that the horses, carts and people could walk along and not be seen from the Hall. Miss Watt gave the orders for this to be done so that her view was not obstructed from the north entrance to Speke Church.

We now come to the main drive to Speke Hall called the Walk and continue alongside Stockton Wood to the North Lodge. Mr and Mrs Youd lived here. He had been an outside worker for some years and by 1932 he had become Head-Gardener. The return walk is now through Stockton Wood.

The following was told to me when I was a young boy. It may have been told to stop me going to the pond in the winter when it was frozen over. The pond was just off the Walk in Stockton Wood, about half way down. It was about 40ft in diameter and was said to be very deep in the centre. The water was black and always seemed to have dead leaves all round the edge. It was stagnant and there was no life in it.

Banks Lane Ha-Ha

North Lodge

Sometime in the 19th century, on a moonlight night in winter, a boy from the village was skating across this pond and the ice in the centre was not as thick as he had thought. The surface cracked and he went under the ice and disappeared. The body was never found, but it was said that when the pond was frozen over the boy appeared skating on the pond. His name was Frank White, son of Moses and Ann White, and was born in 1873. On his gravestone in Speke churchyard is inscribed 'Their son who was accidentally drowned while skating February 21st 1888 aged 15 years'. This is the boy who was drowned in the pond just off the Walk at Speke Hall.

I could never bring myself to go near it. On dark nights as I rode home to the Hall along the Walk I always put a spurt on when I passed this pond, and usually whistled and sang. I never saw anything but the thought was always there.

During World War II, in about 1942, when aircraft were parked in clearings in Stockton Wood, the pond was filled in and the ground levelled off. After this the drive did not seem so sinister. Perhaps the boy's ghost had at last been put to rest.

By entering the wood at the north end, and walking through the centre to a path at the south end one came back to the Walk. This was always pleasant and interesting at any time of the year.

Stockton Wood

I can remember walking through the crunching snow over the dried bracken, with the trees standing up bare against the white snow. In the spring I remember Rhododendron in bloom and the first green of the trees.

In the summer the ground could be hard in the dry weather. The bracken was green and the sun shone through the leaves of the trees. In autumn the fallen leaves lay thick on the ground and we shuffled our feet through them.

On the way out of the wood at the south end we used to pass by the gamekeeper's hut. This hut was used by the gamekeepers to watch over the pheasants. Alongside this hut was a frame not unlike goal posts with a cross bar. On this bar was always hanging an assortment of vermin, or what the gamekeepers called vermin. These included stoat's, weasels, hawks, kestrels, crows, rooks, rats, or anything that would attack the young pheasants.

Coming out of the wood on to the Walk and directing our steps towards the Hall we saw, on the left-hand side, running parallel with the wood, a stream in which all kinds of life abounded. With an old jam-jar we could catch water boatmen, water beetle, caddis fly etc. Today as one continues towards the Hall taking the road round to the left one passes by a beech tree, on the side of which are carved the initials T. W., (executed about 1938-39.) At the end of this road is Home Farm.

Across the small paddock is the main farmhouse. In one of the end four rooms I was born. The bailiff also lived in part of this house. His name was George Wilkin, and he remained bailiff until 1929. The farm was then rented off to William McIndoe. His family was still running the farm in 2000.

Carl Brisson was a Danish entertainer in the 1930s. He began his career as a dancer and singer in Copenhagen nightclubs in 1916, the year after he won Central Europe's amateur middleweight boxing championship. He moved to the London stage in 1923. He appeared in a number of silent movies in the 1920s.

In April 1931 he was appearing in *The Merry Widow* at the Liverpool Empire. He had a caravan in the paddock (now called the orchard), in front of the bailiff's house, (having had permission by the farmer Mr. Bill McIndoe). He returned to the caravan every night after his performance. He had with him two dogs, which had the run of the paddock alongside the caravan. One day when I was walking about I came across a dog collar. I took it to the caravan and gave it to Carl Brisson who thanked me and gave me a signed photograph of himself. My name appears on the back of the photograph.

Carl Brisson and his dogs

PHOTO:
DOROTHY WILDING

CARL BRISSON.

261.R.
BEAGLES POSTCARDS

The back bridge is now a filled in road, leading to the back yard. At the top of the bridge to the right is a plantation with three horse-chestnut trees growing in it. During the autumn when these trees dropped their nuts, known to all young boys as conkers, they would be collected by us to sell to the local boys for one old penny per dozen.

Going over this bridge reminds me of the time we used an old invalid chair as a chariot. We had found it in one of the outhouses over the boiler house. We pulled the chariot to the top of the bridge and after climbing aboard we let it run down this incline into the back yard. This chair had belonged to Miss Watt in the early 1920s. It has since been renovated and was on show in the Large Vehicle Museum in Liverpool.

The Back Bridge

Miss Watt's Invalid Chair

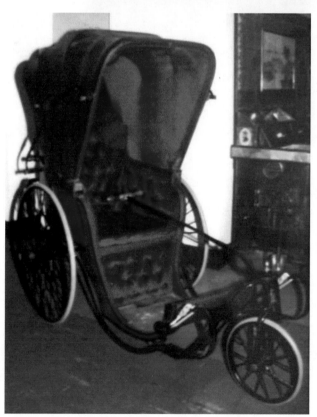

The chair in 1990

Home Farm buildings

CHAPTER 4

"A GENTLEMAN'S COUNTRY ESTATE"

Speke Hall Home Farm was another area of interest to us boys and we would visit it at every available opportunity.

The farm buildings are made of sandstone and date from the Victorian age. They are built in the shape of two 'U's. In the first 'U' on the left are the stables, with the tackle room at one end and two looseboxes at the other end. At the top was the cowshed, used as such until 1930, whilst on the right was the access to the loft, the dairy, blacksmiths shop, and two more looseboxes.

Each morning I would collect a pint of milk from the dairy. It was in the can I had already taken up to the farm the night before. The milk had come straight from the cow through the water cooler and into the can. Milk not used on the estate was put into milk churns and sold to a dairy in Garston.

In the smithy next door, I have watched the smith shoeing the horses. He would first take off the old shoe, then, taking a new and prepared shoe, he would check it for size against the hoof. It was then put into the furnace and after air had been blown into the furnace, the shoe became red hot. After the red-hot shoe had been dipped into a bucket of water to cool, it was then applied to the hoof. I can still recall the smell of the burning hoof, which was then nailed on. The edges were then filed and the hoof completely cooled.

Tackle Room

The water trough made of stone in the centre of the yard was where the horses always took a drink after the day's labour and before they went into the stable for their evening feed.

The Granary

At the top end of the yard, extending from the cowshed on the right over the cartshed is the granary. On each side it has wooden partitioned bays in which was stored the wheat, corn and Indian corn for feeding the animals.

At the end, there was a room where the Irish labourers lived. The room was equipped with straw mattresses on wooden bunks and had a small wood burning cast iron stove. The smell of frying bacon still comes back to me when I think of this room.

Under the granary was the cartshed, which is open at the front and cast iron columns to hold up the floor above. Between these columns the carts were stored. I can remember these carts being painted each year in bright colours.

At the end of the cartshed was a room with a wood fired cast iron boiler. In this boiler the feed for the pigs and chickens was cooked. This consisted of swede, potatoes, grain and bran, all mashed together to form the feed.

Opposite, across the road, was the sawmill. An engine drove the large circular saw. This engine was a Hornsby 'Akroyd' 12 1/2 BHP horizontal stationary engine costing £212 and was installed in 1894. The drive shaft ran under the road to the mixer room. Shafting was also fitted at that time to belt-drive the machine. I can remember seeing this engine running in the 1920s.

This diesel engine also drove a circular saw in the sawmill adjacent to the engine house. By 1939 electricity had been installed in the farm and the line shafting was then driven by an electric motor. The circular saw was used for cutting wood for fence and gateposts and for other work on the estate.

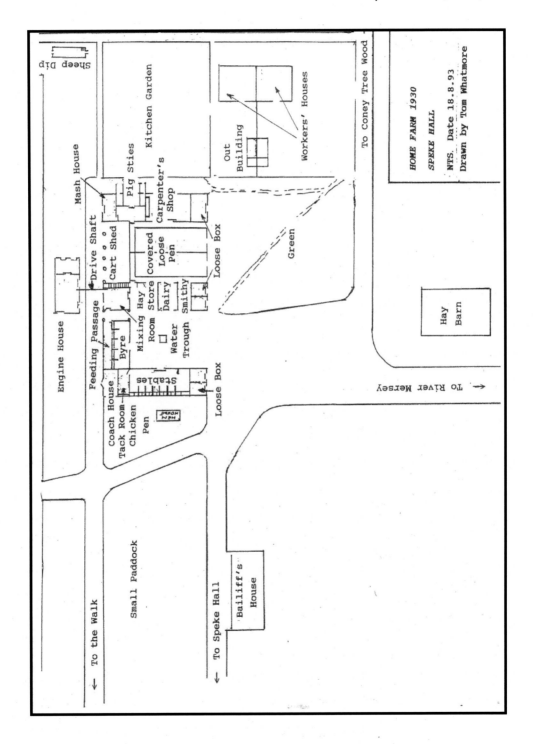

HOME FARM 1930
SPEKE HALL
NTS. Date 18.8.93
Drawn by Tom Whatmore

Running from the cartshed to form a second yard were the pigsties and the carpenter's shop. In this shop the carpenter, Eli, Warren, worked until 1929. He then moved to the old stables by the Hall. When I think of the pigsties, I can hear the noise of the pigs feeding, and smell the odour.

It was in these buildings that I spent a lot of my spare time, playing and exploring. There was always something to see and do, be it bringing the cows in for milking or feeding the pigs, harnessing the horses, feeding the chickens or collecting eggs etc.

The Home Farm Pigsties

The highlight of the year was haymaking. After the grass had been cut with a horse-drawn reaper and left to dry for some days, we would go out with the horse and cart to the field. The cart was long and flat with a high frame at each end. The grass had become hay and it was loaded onto the cart with pitchforks. It was the young helpers' job to tread the hay down and see that it was level. When the cart was full it was taken back to the open barn so that the hay could be stacked. Great care was taken to see that the hay was dry. As the stack was built a steel rod was placed through it. The reason for this was to test the temperature of the stack. There was always the danger of slow combustion and then full fire. On these hot summer evenings to quench our thirst, a barrel of cider would be placed at the end of the field. This made the work much more pleasant to do.

At the end of August the reaping of the wheat and corn would start. The horse-drawn reaper cut the produce of the field and tied it up with string. The produce came out of the reaper in sheaves. These would be set up in the field in stooks to dry. The sheaves would be collected from of the field and taken to the barnyard. Here the process of threshing took place.

Specialist operators usually owned the threshing machine. A threshing machine was driven by a steam engine, connected together by a long drive belt. This process of threshing was very labour intensive. It would require at least six people to control the complete operation.

The produce, wheat or corn, was thrown from the cart to the top of the thresher. It was then fed into the jaws at the top and pushed down. After a process of shaking and racking, the straw came out of the back in wired-up bales. The grain was shaken out of the front and collected in sacks. The chaff dropped out of the bottom into more sacks.

As this procedure continued, the bales of straw were taken and stacked in the barn. The grain was taken to the granary and emptied into one of the bays. The chaff was taken to the loft over the shippen to be stored for bedding or animal feed.

During the cutting of the corn or wheat, as the area to be cut receded, the animal life living in the field migrated to the centre. It was then that the farmer invited his friends to come and join him. They would stand at each corner of the uncut portion of the field. As the rabbits, hares, etc came running out the sport would begin and they blazed away with their 12 bore shotguns.

The Farm Cottages (1930s)

1. George Harland,   cowman
2. Richard Pearson,   cowman.

Alongside the farm green there were two cottages, the one on the right hand side being occupied by George and Mary Harland. They had two sons Leslie and Reg. George Harland was the Cowman.

In order that the two sons, Leslie and Reg could have more free time to accompany us on our exploits around the farm, my brother and I would help them with their daily chores. After the threshing, when the straw bales had been stacked in the barn we would make dens out of straw. As we moved the bales, rats came out, which we chased with sticks and killed.

In the summer months we would collect potatoes from the field and cook them in a biscuit tin lid with some lard over a fire.

As the Hall was occupied until 1921, the farm was run as a home farm for the Hall. The bailiff was George L Wilkin. Between 1926 and 1929 the farm was gradually run down and in 1929 an auction was held to sell off the animals, machinery and carts.

*Old Farm Buildings
(1929)*

From 1930 the home farm was leased to Mr. William McIndoe. A new and modern shippen to accommodate 42 milking cows was built in the area of the covered loose pen. These cows were milked twice a day by hand. It is interesting to note that when the cows came into the shippen from the field they went to what they recognized as their own places.

The looseboxes were used to house cows in calf, and subsequently the mothers and calves, including the young calves that had to be hand reared.

After the milking, the milk was taken to the dairy. Here it was passed through a water cooler and muslin strainer into a milk churn. The milk was then sold to a large commercial dairy for further processing before being sold to the public.

Also in the dairy was a large sink in which were washed the churns. There was also a slatted top table for drying the churns after washing.

The smithy was in full use up to 1938. It was fully equipped with tools, an anvil, bellows and furnace. The blacksmith visited the farm as required from the smithy in Smithy Lane, Speke. The shire horses had to be shod outside in the yard.

A full-time carpenter was employed on the estate and worked from the carpenters shop. His job was to repair the carts, gates, fences and buildings.

The fields were used for grazing the cattle, growing wheat, corn, barley, potatoes, swedes or turnips as well as cabbages. The wheat, corn and barley were stored in the granary. The potatoes were placed in a potato clamp.

A potato clamp is a long shallow trench about 4ft wide with an airshaft. The potatoes are piled to a height of 3ft in the trench and covered with a 6inch layer of straw, beneath a 6inch layer of packed earth. A twist of straw is introduced through the top of the clamp at intervals to ventilate it.

Horse Drawn Reaping Machine

After the day's work the horses went back to the stables first via the water trough in the yard where they took a long drink. They then went into the stables each to its own stall. At the left-hand end of the stable was a larger stall for a mother and foal. There was little change in the farming procedure at the home farm before 1945.

In 1945 the entire herd of accredited cattle was sold and a herd of attested Ayrshire cattle was brought from Scotland. By 1949 the stock was homebred and was developing an excellent strain.

The senior stock bull was the massive beast called Auchenbrian Brass Keys, a three year old that had come to the farm as a yearling and is reported to have done some excellent work. Also coming into use was a 14-month-old Bargower bred bull by the name of Sparnell Bank Hurricane. By 1949 the majority of the herd consisted of heifers, numbering about 40 milkers with 50 young stock excellently housed. The herd was one of the first to become attested in the Liverpool area. The milking was done by machinery and the latest cooling system was employed.

The following records were published in the *Preston Guardian* of Saturday June 25th 1949.

It is recorded that at this time the milk yield was remarkable. In the latest published records for the county (1949) the herd was recorded as being among the leaders of their class. In the one twelve month period of 1949, 26,000 gallons of milk had come from this unit, going mainly to hospitals under contract. And it was hoped that an output of 3.000 gallons of T. T. milk a month would be reached in the near future.

Tea in the old Cow Byre

In the new Shippen for 40 milking cows

At this time a large proportion of the feedstuffs came from the home farmland. The farm as a general rule worked 30 acres of hay, with a second crop for silage for winter feed, balanced with 7 acres of kale, 34 of mixed corn, 24 of oats, 9 of barley, all in addition to normal grazing.

The rest of the acreage of the farm was used for 3,600 dozen broccoli all graded and crated, and over 3,000 40lb bags of peas for tinning.

In 1949 the National Farmers Union arranged a visit to two farms in the Speke area. One was to the Tewit Hall Farm run by Mr. J. T. Chritchley and the other was to the home farm of Speke Hall run by Mr. W. F. McIndoe.

The visitors to each of the farms included the Lord Mayor and Lady Mayoress of Liverpool (Alderman and Mrs. J. J. Cleary), who were accompanied by 50 representatives of the City's municipal and business life.

At the home farm they had tea in the old cow byre and visited the new cow shippen, which housed 40 milking cows. They also visited other parts of the farm.

In the yard outside the Stables and old Cow Byre

By 2008 the old cow byre had become a kitchen, the stables a restaurant and the cow shippen an open space without a roof.

As we come away from the farm along the lower road, we pass the main farmhouse, and the kitchen garden. It is from this garden, throughout the years, that the Hall was provided with fresh vegetables and fruit. This supply of fresh vegetables and fruit continued during our time.

Next to the gardens are the stables, later used by the carpenter Eli Warren. He was continually employed in repairing the woodwork around the Hall. I have watched him, for many hours using all the old carpenters' tools.

ELI JOHN WARREN

Eli Warren lived in 16 Brunswick Street, Garston and would cycle to the Hall every morning for 8am.

He repaired and replaced all the wood in and around the Hall and grounds. His last job was to make a finial for the gable end over the nursery on the south side. This would have been in 1934 when he was in his seventies. I can remember him carving this finial out of a solid piece of oak. He used the old type of tools to fashion it, a hammer and chisel, adze and wood-plane. Although he was over seventy he then went up the thirty foot ladder and fixed it to the apex of the gable-end.

Unfortunately not long after that he collapsed while at work and had to be taken home. In 1935 he died, at the age of 73 years.

In 1919 his weekly wage at the Hall was £3.13s.1d.

Brunswick Street, Garston

Brunswick Street was built with the backs of the houses to the road and the fronts looking towards Speke Hall. I was always told that this had been done on the orders of Adelaide Watt. It was said, that she gave this order, because she did not want to see the washing on the lines from the Hall. This story became part of Garston folklore. As these houses were built in 1865 for the Welsh workers from the Bibby's Copper Works, Garston and in 1865 Adelaide would then have been only eight years old, I do not think that she gave this order. The land on which Brunswick Street is built was part of the Speke Hall estate and was called in the field list of 1781 'Garston Hay'.

SHOOTING DAYS

Each year as far back as I can remember, (certainly until 1939) a shoot was organised on the estate. From November to the end of January shooting would take place all day on a Saturday at least twice a month and sometimes on Boxing Day.

In the 1920s the shoots were leased to a Mr. Cockran and in the 1930s to Mr. Leather.

Arrangements for the shoots started in April each year. At this time it was the gamekeeper's job to collect, from the Clough Wood and Stockton Wood, pheasant's eggs laid by the wild birds, which had avoided being shot the previous year. Frank and I would help them to do this by searching under the Rhododendron bushes in the woods. We usually found 10 to 12 eggs per nest. The pheasant's eggs are uniformly pale, an olive-brown shade, not unlike a hen's egg, but smaller.

These eggs were placed in coops under broody hens, about 6 eggs to each hen. Clough Field was used for this. The gamekeeper's stayed on guard. They even slept in their wooden hut in the field. They did this to prevent any interference with the young birds from vermin or vandals.

When the young birds had hatched out they were looked after by the hens for about 6 weeks. They were then taken into different sections of the Clough Wood and Stockton Wood.

Each day these young birds had to be fed. Their food was prepared by boiling potatoes and grain in a big iron cauldron over a wood fire by the gamekeeper's hut in Stockton Wood. When the feed was cooked and cool it was taken to the young birds in the woods. This was to get the birds accustomed to a daily feed, and thus keep them in that section of the wood.

During the summer months the young birds grew into fine pheasants. The cock bird grew to some 33 inches long and was very colourful. It had a distinctive red eye patch on a black head and neck. The hen, on the other hand, was about 23 inches long and mottled brown. The pheasant does not pair off. I have frequently seen, in the spring, groups of cock birds, collecting and consorting together without a single hen.

The pheasant-shooting season starts on the 1st October and ends on the 31st January. However I do not remember any shoots starting before November on the Speke estate.

The day of a shoot would start with the beaters collecting at the Hall in the back yard. They were usually men from the farms on the estate or from Speke village. The dog handlers and loaders would arrive and, to complete the party, the shooters would arrive in estate cars. They went straight to the gunroom in the west wing of the Hall. Here they assembled their 12 bore shot guns, filled their leather bags with cartridges and had a drink before going out to their different stations for the shoot.

Meanwhile the beaters had made their way to the north end of Stockton Wood under the direction of George Boult.   Here they lined up across the wood, about 15 to 20 feet apart.

They walked slowly through the wood, beating the ground on each side with their sticks, shouting all the time. As they approached the south end the pheasants got up and flew over the trees. The beaters now shouted, "cock over!" This prepared the guns, and they blazed away at the birds. Some birds got away and flew to the Clough Wood where they would ensure the afternoons shooting. Shot birds were collected by the gun dogs and brought to a position at the end of Banks Lane.

It was Frank's and my job to collect these birds, brace them and tie up cock and hen together using sisal or baling twine, to a length of about 12inches. They were subsequently hung on the side of a horse-drawn float and taken to the old dairy at the Hall and suspended there for about a week. Then they were sold off to defray the cost of the next shoot.

After the morning shoot lunch was taken. The shooting party came into the Hall to the Blue Drawing Room. Here my father served them their meal. They started their meal by having sherry, then a hot soup, followed by hotpot and biscuits and cheese. The drink during the meal would be whisky and soda, followed by port or brandy. This meal could last over an hour. I can remember checking the empty bottles and testing what had been left in them.

The dog handlers and loaders had their meal in the kitchen, and the beaters had theirs in the old stables or the washhouse. Their meal consisted of a large meat pie and bread and cheese all washed down with a large bottle of Worthington's beer per man.

After the meal, the beaters went to the south end of Clough Wood on the shoreline and beat through to the south lawn. By this time the guns had positioned themselves in the west moat and south lawn. The birds came out, followed by the beaters emitting the usual shout. The birds' chances of survival were greatly affected by the amount of liquid refreshment consumed during the lunch break. Failing light was another important factor in their possible survival.

In my recollection, the days always seemed to be bright and dry with a frosty morning and a bright afternoon. Sometimes there was snow on the ground. They were pleasant and happy days. Each year the shooting days were dates on the calendar, which my brother and I would look forward to.

As a result of the day's activities we could always be sure of having pheasant on the menu for our next Sunday lunch.

GEORGE BOULT

George Boult lived in one of the cottages on Oglet Lane, and was the head game keeper at the Hall while we lived there. He was a man of over 6ft in height. He always dressed in plus fours, wide knickerbockers, a heavy tweed coat and a cap. He carried a stout stick in one hand and a twelve bore shotgun under his other arm. He was always accompanied by a dog. He was not a person to trifle with, as many a poacher learnt to his cost.

His duties were to rear and look after the pheasants and to keep the vermin at bay. This would involve shooting or trapping weasels, stoats, rats, crows, hawks, kestrels, owls, etc. He would hang them on a frame made of wood, (looking like goal posts). This frame was placed by the gamekeeper's hut in Stockton Wood. The hanging vermin on this frame proved that he was keeping the vermin down.

In 1919 his weekly wage at the Hall was £2.13s.0d.

Part of Speke Hall Estate (1931)

CHAPTER 5

THE COMING OF THE AIRPORT 1928-1964

On the 1st August 1926 Liverpool City Council decided to purchase part of the Speke estate, from the executors of its former owner, Miss Adelaide Watt. The sum of £162 was paid for the land. More land was bought in 1933.

The building of Speke Airport started about March 1930. The first aerodrome licence was granted on the 16th June 1930, and on that day the first arrival of an Armstrong Whitworth Argosy airliner of Imperial Airways landed. It was not until after the official opening of the Airport in July 1933 that a regular service was operated.

During 1931 and 1932 further levelling of the site was authorised with use of Chapel House as the terminal building and offices.

On the 6th July 1932 Captain H. J. Andrews was appointed airport manager, with a salary of £400 a year.

I can remember these dates very well. It was a time when Banks Lane was being closed; the hawthorn hedges dug up and ponds filled in with old refuse after the water had been pumped out. I was able to see fish and eels in the mud on the bottom and collected some of them for my aquarium in the old washhouse. I remember the first aircraft landing. Great squares were whitewashed on the grass to mark out the landing area.

Thoughout these activities Banks Lane was still open to us. It was our main way to Garston and to school and it affected access for supplies to be delivered to the Hall. The postman came this way every morning to bring the post and the daily papers. By 1933 the lane was closed and our route was then via Baileys Lane and the north lodge.

By 1934, both Banks Lane and Baileys Lane had been closed and our route to Garston was now via Speke Hall Avenue, which added two miles on to our journey. By 1937 the main hangar and control tower had been completed and opened.

By 1936 the airport had been extended over Baileys Lane making a vast open space. It was then said to be the third busiest aerodrome in Great Britain.

During 1936, the official records indicated 18,489 landings by aircraft and a similar number of departures, involving the carriage of 111,700 persons and 1,900,871 lbs of mails and freight. This showed an increase over the figures for 1935.

A complete installation for the illumination of the airport for night flying had been erected, said to be to be the finest of its kind yet produced, and utilising four floodlights of 1,750,000 candle power each, which literally turned night into day so far as the 400 acres of landing area was concerned.

The largest aeroplane hangar in the United Kingdom had been erected, together with a control tower of the most modern type. A station building adjoining the main hangar for the convenient handling of the passenger traffic was by then nearing completion.

The internal activity of the airport had been augmented by the formation of the County of Lancashire No 611 Bomber Squadron of the Auxiliary Air Force, which had established its headquarters at the airport.

It was generally felt at that time, that developments should proceed to ensure that the airport would possess all the qualities outlined in the then Maybury Report, which suggested to the Government the necessity for a northern junction airport equipped for all-weather flying and landing in fog. The vicar of Garston was appointed chaplain to the R. A. F. squadron.

The vicar of Speke wrote at that time, *"The pastoral care of the officers and men is in the hands of the vicar of Garston, and so does not come within the privileges and duties of the vicar of this parish. Nevertheless any of the officers and men and their families who are stationed here will find a ready welcome in the church of All Saints Speke".*

On June 11th 1937, the operation of the airport was transferred from the temporary building at Chapel House to the new hangar and control tower. The new hangar represented the most advanced practices and was the largest civil hangar available for aeroplanes. The tower was fully equipped with every modern device in existence at that time. This enhanced the safety of the traveller by air. A new and experimental radio beacon had been put into operation, which rendered the landing of aircraft under conditions of dense fog, not only possible, but also consistently safe.

In September 1939 the airport was requisitioned, and was occupied by 24 Hampdens of 61 and 144 squadrons. They did not stay long at Speke. On the night of 16th September 1940 bombs were dropped rendering the base unserviceable.

Four fatalities occurred among men of the Royal Engineers who were defusing an unexploded bomb.

On June 17th 1940, Lysanders of 13 Squadron came to Speke and stayed for about a month.

Hurricanes of the 312 Czech Squadron followed the Lysanders, and, on the 8th October 1940, they claimed the fastest 'kill' of the Second World War. The destruction of a Junkers J U 88 was achieved by three Hurricanes in less than eight minutes from take-off to touch down. The mission of the Junkers had been to bomb the Rootes aircraft factory on the edge of the airport. The fighters were scrambled just in time to cause the J U. 88 to crash land at Bromborough on the opposite bank of the Mersey. On December 17th 1940, Czech President Benes inspected the squadron and its aircraft and a month later the Duke of Kent carried out another inspection. The squadron left for Valley in March 1941.

It was replaced by the Polish 315 Squadron, which soon became operational and began convoy patrols over Liverpool Bay.

The airport was selected on the 4th May 1941 as the base for the "Merchant Ship Fighter Unit". This had an establishment of 56 Hurricanes. A catapult was positioned in front of hangar 2 and aimed towards the river. The first rocket launch took place on July 6th. The unit was disbanded on September 7th 1943.

Throughout the war all types of military aircraft were stationed at Speke. The airport was used by the Lockheed Company to overhaul and assemble some 2.690 U.S.A.A.F. aircraft including large numbers of P-38 Lightning's, P-47s and P-51s. P-61 Black Widows arrived in 1944.

At the end of the war the flow of new aircraft from the USA was reversed as hundreds of fighters passed through in preparation for the return voyage.

THE VANISHING LADY

An interesting occurrence took place in 1933 after the Liverpool City had purchased the land for the building of the airport. The hawthorn hedges had been dug up on each side of Banks Lane. Only the fields on one side of the road were being used for landing aircraft. Chapel House Farm, set about 200 yards in towards the river from Banks Lane was in use as a control tower and reception for the airport. Banks Lane had not yet been closed as a right of way between the Hall and Garston. To get home from school I had to ride along this lane, past Chapel House Farm and Sutton Grange.

One afternoon in September about 4pm, I was returning home to the Hall. The weather was clear, as it had been a sunny day. On passing Chapel House I saw what appeared to be a figure dressed in a black suit. The figure was walking towards me along Banks Lane. I rode past the figure and saw that it was a lady dressed in a black serge suit. I did not recognise the lady. After I had ridden about hundred yards or so, I looked round and the figure had disappeared. She may have gone into the farm, but I do not think so. She had not had time to get that far.

I would then have been 11 years old, and did not think any more about this strange occurrence. Over the last few years, since I have been thinking about my past, the thought has come to me, that, perhaps, the figure I saw that afternoon in 1933 was an impression of Miss Watt.

Maybe she was disturbed about the way the estate was being sold off and broken up. I travelled this way four times each day over the next two years, until Banks Lane was closed to all traffic. I did not see this figure again, or anyone that could have resembled her.

***

In July 1933 during the official opening of the airport, we had a grandstand seat alongside the buildings of Sutton Grange. It was on this side of the airport that the aircraft came to be refuelled. We were able to closely inspect them as they arrived throughout the day. It is said that this pageant was the greatest air display ever held outside of Hendon at that time.

Captain Andrews in 1935 invited me to fly with him in a small biplane to Blackpool. This was on a Saturday afternoon. I can remember flying over Liverpool and seeing football matches being played. I would then have been 13 years old. However this was not my first flight, as I had been taken up in 1933 in a passenger plane on a 5 shillings flight.

A most important event took place in 1937 for the people of Liverpool, Garston and Speke. Rootes Motor Group built a shadow aircraft factory. This factory gave work to many thousands of people on Merseyside.

It was built on land that had been part of the Speke Hall estate between the North Lodge and All Saints Church Speke. During building Hall Lane was closed which added an extra mile to our journey to Speke Church.

The shadow factory was built to produce Bristol Blenheim fighter-bombers. The first plane produced flew in October 1938. This I can remember seeing. The

Handley Page Halifax Bomber

last Blenheim flew out on November 1941. A total of 2,480 aircraft were produced during this time. It was not until April 1942 that Speke produced another aircraft. On this date the first Handley Page Halifax bomber flew. A total of 1,070 Halifax bombers were built at Speke between 1942 and July 1945.

Speke Township Map (1932)

Military aircraft landing and taking off from Speke Airport necessitated that Clough Wood be cut down. Thus a beautiful wood was spoiled.

Speke Airport, Chapel House (1932)

CHAPTER 6

SPEKE HALL IN WAR 1939-1945

In September 1939 we had to prepare the Hall for war. This meant installing blackout facilities. We found it impossible to cover all the windows, so we concentrated, therefore, on windows in those rooms actively being used. These were the butler's pantry, housekeeper's room and bedrooms. We had to use a torch to light our way from room to room. We also prepared a makeshift shelter under the back stairs. The shelter consisted of a mattress on a table. At the start of the war, at the sound of the air raid alarm, we would, at once, retire to this shelter. But as the first alarms were all false, it was not used seriously until May 1940.

When the war started I was 17 years old, and was a member of a civil defence unit stationed in the new housing estate in Speke. I served as a messenger, going from station to station on my bicycle; I was equipped with gas mask and tin hat and wore my scout uniform. It was exiting for the first few months of the war.

After the evacuation from Dunkirk in June 1940, we had a number of evacuated soldiers stationed at the Hall. They camped in bell-tents in Stockton Wood, and used the old stables as a cookhouse. By the autumn of that year they had been re-equipped and moved away.

We had a number of anti-aircraft guns stationed around the Hall. One of these was in the Park Field on the north side. In October 1940 after the nights raid, the gun crew was busy cleaning their guns, when a German Junkers JU88 came over Liverpool on a reconnaissance mission. The 312 Hurricane Squadron from Speke took off and shot it down. It crashed landed at Bromborough on the opposite side of the Mersey. This aircraft was put on show in Liverpool on St Georges Plateau. I saw this dogfight taking place, which resulted in the plane being shot down and landing.

During the May blitz of Liverpool in 1940, we could see the German planes over the town, the bombs exploding and Liverpool burning. Fortunately at the Hall,

all we had was one bomb dropped in the Park Field and a few incendiary bombs, which fortunately all fell in the fields around.

On the 9th of April 1942 I joined the Home Guard. Our headquarters was in Kingsthorne Road School, Hunts Cross. I was on duty on Monday and Tuesday nights of each week and quite often at a weekend. I qualified as a trained man on the 11th May, and was fully equipped on the 28th May.

The Home Guard of South Liverpool had a hand grenade range extending from the bottom of Clough Field, down on to the Mersey shore. They also used the shore for firing the Northover-projectors. This was a 3inch drainpipe mounted on a carriage with a firing pin at the loading end. The projectile was a bottle of phosphorus, serving as an anti-tank weapon. It was never used in anger.

During the years 1942-44 Lockheed Hudsons and other aircraft were shipped from America to the Liverpool docks. These aircraft were pulled in convoy through the streets to end up in Stockton Wood. The trees had been cut down to make clearings. To enable these aircraft to be manoeuvred into the entrance at the North Lodge, a road had to be cut across the roundabout. The gates at the Lodge entrance had also to be enlarged. Packing cases of aircraft parts were placed down the Walk.

Road across roundabout (1960s)

Speke Hall was now a military zone and guards were stationed at the North Lodge and around the complete estate. We had to report to these guards on entering and leaving the Hall.

In time, the guards got to know us and would let us in without any check. However after some months the guards were changed, and as I returned home one night I was stopped and asked for my identity card. Unfortunately, on this occasion I did not have it with me. As I could not convince the guards that I was going home I was arrested. They marched me off to the guardhouse, which was in the control tower at the airport. I was kept there about one hour and, after making some phone calls, I managed to convince the officer that I was really going home and was then allowed to go free.

These aircraft were taken from the woods to the hangars at the airport, to be assembled by the R.A.F. They were then flown off to other operation bases.

Tom Whatmore, Scoutmaster (1942)

Tom Whatmore. Home Guard (1942)

101

MY FIRST CAR

1932 Standard 9 Car

This picture was taken at the top of the back bridge at Speke Hall 1944.

In the summer of 1944 I was able to purchase a 1932 Standard 9 at a cost of £50. I was able to do this because my work at that time ensured that I attained a small ration of petrol.

The car had been laid up in a garage because of the war and lack of petrol. It had been well looked after and the owner had lifted it up on house bricks to save the tyres and had turned the engine over from time to time.

After purchase we lowered the car off the bricks and inflated the tyres and put petrol in the tank. Then, with a tow, the engine started and I was able to take the car home to Speke Hall.

After some practice driving up and down the drive at the Hall I was able to take it out on the roads. This was no problem as there were very few cars on the road at that time.

I kept and ran this car until 1950 and then sold it for £100.

CHAPTER 7

THE SPEKE TOWNSHIP 1920 TO 1946

A township is a division of a large parish and manor, containing a village.

Speke Village (1932)

The township of Speke in 1926 extended from the Mersey along Brunswick Street, up Banks Road, Garston out towards Speke, through the railway sidings on its north side, to Hillfoot Road and Hillfoot Avenue, Hunts Cross, then through the fields to Dungeon Lane on its east side, to Hale and the Mersey. The Mersey was the boundary of the township on the south side between Hale and Garston. It covered an area of 2379 acres. Within this acreage was the Speke Hall estate, taking up a total area of 843 acres. Brunswick Street, Banks Road, Baileys Lane, and Hall Road bounded the estate, through the fields past Tewit Hall Farm to Oglet Lane and the Mersey.

Mr. Corn's House, Smithy Lane

The River Mersey's shoreline between Garston and Oglet was generally sandy with high banks to the fields, and a walk along the top. At low water the sand banks could be seen. The fishing boats came from Garston to fish as far up the Mersey as Oglet. Fish were caught there until the early 1940s. In one of the cottages of Oglet Lane lived an old man who used to catch shrimps in the river and go round the district selling them from a huge basket covered with a snow-white cloth.

I can remember an incident in the 1930s when one of these fishing boats capsized near Speke Hall. The fisherman came up to the Hall to get help. My father supplied him with dry clothes and a fire was lit in the washhouse stove to dry his clothes.

Yewtree Farm, Oglet Lane

Mr. Bennet's Farm, Speke Town

The land of the township was generally used for farming. There were nine farms, four woods and over one hundred ponds. The estate had three farms, four woods and over forty ponds.

The township had a village, church school, post office, smithy, two general shops run from the front rooms of the house, a vicarage and about thirty houses.

Within the township were woods called Sutton, Little Heath, Dam and Grace's. On the Estate were the Clough, Stockton, Gunning Tree or Coney Tree, (Rabbit Wood) and Cartwright's Plantation.

All the woods of the township have now been removed to make way for the new housing estate and the 1970 runways of Liverpool Airport.

The Coney Tree Wood has also been destroyed to make way for this runway. This was not far up from the Home Farm and was one of the woods we played in.

All the main roads fanned out from the church at the centre of the township. In a northerly direction was Speke Church Road to Speke Village; it subsequently ran into Woodend Lane and Hunts Cross. Going east was Hale Road with Oglet Lane and Dungeon Lane running off it before going on to Hale Village. Going south was Hall Lane, which went to the North Lodge and Baileys Lane, and Garston.

A minor road came off the end of Banks Road and went to Speke Hall. This road was called Banks Lane. From Banks Lane one saw Chapel House on the right and, half way along, Sutton Grange, also on the right. One passed the West Lodge on the right and the dam on the left and eventually, arrived at the Walk.

Sutton Grange was the estate house and office. The estate agent was Mr. R. Ashby Graves. The house was closed in 1926 and, by 1936, had been demolished to make way for Liverpool Airport.

Sutton Grange was a very big estate house complete with stables, coach house, and out-houses for servants. It was situated midway between the West Lodge and Chapel House Farm on Banks Lane. Banks Lane ran between the Walk, past the dam to Banks Road, Garston.

Butcher's Lane was very short and ran off Speke Church Road on the left, opposite the church. It is said that the 'Greyhound' pub had been in this Lane. Miss Watt closed this Hostelry in 1878. Also in this lane was the parish mortuary. Drowned men found on the river shore were taken there.

On each side of the roads and lanes were high hawthorn hedges, with five barred gates into the fields. Even at a very young age we were not afraid of walking along these roads. They had no lighting and we had to carry a lamp or torch. If we rode our bicycles it was highly probable that we would get a puncture from a thorn shed by the hawthorn hedges. I can remember, in January 1936, having to walk in the evenings one and a half miles from the Hall to the vicarage in Woodend Lane for confirmation classes.

The following is a description that appeared in the Press about 1926:
"Liverpool comes to an untidy end at Garston and peters out soon after you leave the tram lines into a high road lined with hedges. Follow that road but a little way and at 7 miles from the Town Hall, you will find yourself in a quiet little village. For Speke is a quiet spot unless you happen to be there at the weekend when you will find it being used as a busy traffic way." This description was still true in 1929, for then it was still a quiet village.

But in 1929 the untidiness had already crossed the city boundary. The magnificent hedges on the new siding side of Dodds Lane had been ruthlessly uprooted and burnt, to be replaced by a so-called unclimbable iron fence. Behind this fence was a huge shed and railway lines, this work had been done for the L. M .S. railways (London Midland Scottish).

During 1934-35, two new roads were constructed. One from Hunts Cross, this became Speke Hall Road and led into Speke Hall Avenue to the North Lodge. The other, called Speke Road ran from Garston, by Mount Pleasant, to the junction of Speke Hall Road and Speke Hall Avenue. Baileys Lane was closed and taken into the airport area.

Speke Road was constructed in 1935 and ran from Banks Road to the roundabout connection of Speke Hall Road and Speke Hall Avenue. It was made into a dual carriageway, two lanes on each road and was edged by a cycle track. Low lighting columns provided the lighting with sodium lamps. These columns continued round the roundabout and halfway down Speke Hall Avenue. The low lighting was for the safety of the aircraft landing at the airport.

The two thatched cottages at the corner of Speke Town Lane, (5 and 6 Delph Lane) were demolished and the materials used for the foundation of the new roundabout.

DELPH LANE

VANISHING HOMES AT SPEKE TOWN CORNER
5 and 6 Delph Lane.

1. John Reedhind   cowman
2. James Irving   cowman

The Delph, was a disused quarry, which had yielded red sandstone, characteristic of the countryside. This sandstone can be seen in many Liverpool Churches including Speke and the Cathedral. The Delph at one time was used as a rifle range.

The Delph Rifle Range

FOOTPATHS

(1) From Banks Road across the allotment gardens (by Marsh's Farm) coming out on Baileys Lane, at the end of Dodds Lane. This path was very useful to cut off the corner.

(2) From Baileys Lane at the North Lodge, across the field by Stockton Wood, and coming out on Mill Brow. We would use this path if we wanted to go to Oglet.

FARMS

Within the boundaries of the township excluding the estate were the following farms.

NAME	FARMER	LOCATION
Speke Farm	Arthur. H. Barrow	Smithy Lane.
Blacklock Hall	Robert Heathcote Swift	Smithy Lane
Yewtree Farm	Arron Harrison Cartwright	Oglet Lane
Speke Town Farm	James Peacop	Delph Lane
Hale Road Farm	Alfred Sumner	Hale Road
Goldfinch Farm	John Leslie Corlett	Hale Road
Hunts Tenements	William .S. Harrison	Hale Road
Oglet Farm	James Pye	Oglet Lane
Greyhound Farm	Thomas. T. Critchley	Speke Church Road
Woodland Farm		Woodend Lane

Honey Hall Farm	Edward. A. Holme	Woodend Lane
Rose Farm	Williams Family	Near Hunts Cross
Greyhound Farm	William Cartwright	Church Road

On the Estate: -

Tewit Hall	John. Turton Critchley	Oglet Lane
Mount Pleasant	George Given Marsh. J. P.	Baileys Lane
Home Farm	William McIndoe	Speke Hall
Chapel House Farm	Mr. Ball	Banks Lane
Sutton Grange	Mr. A Graves	Banks Lane

HOUSES and COTTAGES

The population of Speke in 1929-30 according to the Census of that date was 366. Each of the 366 was well-known to their fellow residents his or her.

30, 32, 33 Hale Road

HALE ROAD:

30. Roy Simpson	Teams man.
32. Alan Bland	Postmaster.
32. Mrs. Bland	Headmistress
33. Joseph Thomas Whitehouse	Teams man.

Hale Road, cottages were single or twin spread along the road and not numbered.

Arthur Ellison	Engine Man
Thomas Dunbavin	Smallholder
Mrs. Rebecca Southern	Housewife
William Edward Wyke	Teams man
William Hartley	Teams man
William Dutton	Teams man
James Latham	Labourer

WOODEND LANE:

Woodend Cottage

'Woodend':   Mrs. Lizzie. M. Mawdsley   Laundry

SPEKE TOWN LANE:

7, Town Lane

5. Annie Lunt
6. John Crosby — Woodworker
7. George and Eliza Wyke — Teamsman
10. Thomas & Arthur Wyke — Wheelwrights
   John Ireland — Labourer
   Walter and Eliz Handley — Blacksmith
   Richard Green — Labourer *(These were cottages but unnumbered)*
   Richard Owen Jones — Labourer
   John Ball — Labourer
   Thomas Mc Nally — Labourer

SMITHY LANE:

The house of Isaac, Corn Labourer

SPEKE CHURCH ROAD:

16. Aaron Stanley — Labourer
17. Patrick Walsh — Labourer
18. Arthur Worrall — Labourer
19 Peter Prescott — Labourer
20. Herbert Sumner — Shopkeeper
22. Stephen Farr — Labourer

OGLET LANE:

59, 60 Oglet Lane   *57, 58 Oglet Lane*

?	George Boult	Gamekeeper
48.	William Freeman	Labourer
49.	Charles Roberts	Shopkeeper
51a	Albert Southern	Teams man
51.	John Lea, Junr	Teams man
?	James Latham	Gardener
57.	Walter Southern	Gardener
?	Edward Symmons	Gardener
58.	Mrs. Alice Hartley	
59.	Thomas Hulme	Labourer
61.	John Lea	Labourer
55.	Thomas Mercer	Teams man
56.	R. Leadbetter	Labourer

BUTCHERS LANE:

29, 30 Butchers Lane

North Lodge, William Youd, Head Gardener

Poverty Nook, Joseph Barrow, Blacksmith

HALL LANE:

26. George Charles Quint   Joiner/Houseman
25. Frederick. L. Moule   Police

BAILEYS LANE:

8. Edmund Lowndes   Labourer
9. George Sparrow   Labourer

The cottages in Baileys Lane were of the same design as the ones in Hall Lane and Mill Brow. They were situated at Garston at the end of Baileys Lane opposite Mount Pleasant Farm.

MILL BROW:

Joseph Barrow   Smallholder

Joseph Spann   Teams man

The cottages in Banks Lane, Baileys Lane, Hall Lane and Mill Brow were built for estate workers in the time of Adelaide Watt. The cottages in Baileys Lane were demolished for the building of the 1936 airport control tower. Hall Lane cottages were demolished in the 1940s. Those in Mill Brow became derelict in the late

113

1990s and were demolished for the building of the new Liverpool John Lennon Airport. Banks Lane cottages are still occupied 2009.

The architecture and design of all these cottages are all the same; this can be seen in the photographs on page 113 of Mill Brow and Hall Lane. The photographs on this page are of the cottages in Banks Lane, they have been modernised over the years, but they still have the same general design as the other cottages.

BANKS LANE: (Photographs taken 2009)

1.	George Ellison	Labourer (1930s)
3.	Lawrence Harrison	Labourer (1930s)

5. Bonney Francis (1930s)
7. Mrs. Nicholls (1930s)

SPEKE HALL STAFF 1921 TO 1926

BORN	NAME	POSITION	DIED	AGE
	Mr. R Ashby Graves	Estate Agent		
	Mrs. E M Fowler	Estate Secretary		
	Mr. George L Wilkin	Farm Bailiff		
30/5/1880	Mr. Thomas Whatmore	Butler	20/11/1967	87
8/3/1882	Mr. George W Bailey	Chauffeur	17/2/1969	87
	Mr. George Boult	Game-Keeper		
1873	Mr. George Quint	Houseman	5/2/1945	72
1862	Mr. Eli John Warren	Joiner	18//11/1935	73
1871	Mr James Latham	Gardener	15/5/1937	66
1871	Mr. Walter Southern	" "	12/3/1950	79
	Mr Edward Simmons	" "		
1875	Mr. William Youd	" "	30/5/1934	59
1887	Mr. Thomas Whitehouse	Teamster	5/12/1977	90
	Mr Thomas Wyke	Smithy		
	Mr. Arthur Wyke	Wheelwright		
	Miss Beardsmore (Mrs.)	Cook		
	Miss Alice Roberts.	Kitchen Maid		

STAFF 1929

Eli John Warren	Joiner	16 Brunswick Street, Garston
George William Bailey	Chauffeur	67 Speke Road, Garston
George Quint	Houseman	26 Hall Lane, Speke.
George Boult	Game-Keeper	Oglet Lane, Speke.
James Latham	Gardener	Oglet Lane, Speke.
Walter Southern	Gardener	57 Oglet Lane, Speke.
Edward Symmons	Gardener	Oglet Lane, Speke.
William Youd	Gardener	North Lodge, The Walk, Speke Hall.
Joseph Thomas Whitehouse	Teams man	33 Hale Road, Speke.
Roy Simpson	Teams man	32 Hale Road, Speke.
Isaac Corn	Labourer	Smithy Lane, Speke.
Edmond Lowndes	Labourer	Baileys Lane, Speke.
Thomas Wyke	Wheelwright	10 Speke Town Lane, Speke.
Thomas Whatmore	Custodian	Speke Hall.

CHAPTER 8

ALL SAINTS CHURCH SPEKE
and CHURCH SCHOOL

SUNDAYS AT SPEKE HALL 1926-1939

Sunday was a day of rest and we had to consider it as such. We could not play any games but walking in the grounds was quite in order. The start of the day meant dressing in our best clothes and walking for half an hour from the Hall along the Walk and Hall Lane to All Saints Church in Speke Village, for the 11am Service.

The vicar was the Rev L. R. Paterson. Miss Watt had given him the living of All Saints Speke in 1907. It was his custom to arrive at the church riding on his bicycle with an old tweed cape over his shoulders. This cape had seen many years of wear. The bicycle was an old sit-up-and-beg machine with extensions on the rear wheel nuts (called a back step) to enable him to get on to the saddle, which was quite a performance. Holding the handlebars he would run along behind with his left foot on the back-step, his right leg being used to scoot the bicycle along. Eventually he lifted himself on to the saddle and pedalled away. To dismount he would reverse the procedure.

Morning service was taken from the 1662 Prayer Book and the service was always taken complete from that book. It never varied. The vicar's sermons were long and he would continually have a dewdrop on the end of his nose. After the service we would walk home to the Hall and sit down to a good lunch of roast beef accompanied by fresh vegetables from the gardens. The rest of the day was spent

117

either reading or walking in the grounds. Sunday, from morning to evening, was always spent dressed in our best clothes of blue-serge which we wore summer and winter.

At the age of eight Frank, then I, joined the choir and had to go to church three times every Sunday and every Wednesday evening during Lent. In the summer it was a lovely walk but in the winter it could be very bleak, especially at night. In the dark we used a carbide lamp to light the way. This lamp had to be lit by wetting the carbide to make it give off gas, which was then ignited. At times it was difficult to wet the carbide, especially if the light went out when we were on the road. If this happened we had to spit on the carbide. This type of lamp gave a very good light to the front of us but all around would be very dark. We would waste no time in walking down the Walk through Stockton Wood back to the Hall. This would be about eight in the evening.

We would then have supper and go to bed.

A choirboy's pay was two shillings and six pence per quarter with deductions for absence. At 13 or 14 years of age or when the voice broke we had to retire from the choir. During my time in the choir, as a 12 year old, it was my job to light the candles on each side of the pulpit. I had to do this just before the vicar went up to give his sermon. The congregation at the evening service usually consisted of no more than six people, but this did not deter our vicar. He gave his usual sermon of at least half an hour. After the sermon it was my duty to go into the vestry and fetch the snuffer to put out the candles.

As we had no electricity in the church, lighting was by paraffin oil lamps. These had to be cleaned during the week and lit before the evening service. Mr. George Quint did this work.

In 1932 the members of the choir were, Fred Loundes, Eric Coates, Cyril Coates, Derek Farr, Ron Lucas, Tom Whatmore, Reg Harland, Frank Whatmore and Fred Lucas. The choirmaster and organist was Mr. P. H. Blease. Reg Harland had a very good voice and was head boy. He was about three years older than I was and a friend; he was the son of the cowman at Speke home farm.

During the sermon Reg spent his time doing cartoon sketches usually on the back page of the Hymn Book of all the people around him. One of his favourite subjects was the vicar complete with his dewdrop. When we arrived in church one Sunday morning the vicar's wife was asking the choir boys who the artist was. Eventually the name of Reg Harland came out. Reg naturally thought he was for the high jump but much to his surprise, he was congratulated on his drawings and asked to bring more in to show her. Mrs. Paterson, who was very artistic, showed

118

a great interest in Reg. She encouraged him to do more drawings but not of the vicar and not in the hymn books.

Each year the choir was taken on an outing, the cost of which was defrayed by a few of the parishioners. Southport was the usual destination. We would collect together at Hunt's Cross station. Our journey was by steam train, which arrived at Southport about midday. We were taken to lunch and had our photograph taken. The afternoon was taken up by a visit to the fair, followed by a visit to the shops and, to complete the day, afternoon tea was taken. We returned to Hunt's Cross station at about 8 o'clock in the evening, a very tired but happy choir. In later years the trip was to tea in Liverpool and then to a cinema.

In the Speke Parochial Annual of 1937-38 the Vicar writes: *The Sunday afternoon Service for children and their mothers continues to fill the place of a formal Sunday school, and recently a much better attendance has been made than was the case earlier in the year. Some more children from the Speke Estate houses now come regularly, and we hope when the new houses in the centre of the parish are occupied, there will be many more children and their mothers for us to welcome to this service. When children join up they are given an album in which they stick the stamp given at each service, as a record of their attendance, and at the end of the year, children with a complete set of stamps in their albums are rewarded by receiving a little medal.* Some children received their seventh medal at the beginning of Advent, after the Church's year came to an end when it was time to hand in "Albums for inspection". In the years 1928 to 1936 I received eight of these medals.

Speke Church Choir (1932)

119

Speke Church Choir (1940)

Front Row

X X Frank Whatmore X X Rev Wade Mr. Blease X Tom Whatmore X

I have marked with an X for the people I cannot recognise.

By 1937-38 all this had changed, a new housing estate had been built on the Speke estate around the church and a new and larger congregation attended. By then we had a curate, the Rev. W H Wade.

Just after the outbreak of war in September 1939, the vicar L. R. Paterson was killed in an accident in Speke. He was knocked from his bicycle whilst attending to his parish duties. After his death the Rev. W. H. Wade was given the living of All Saints Speke by the trustees of Speke Hall.

VICARS OF THE PARISH 1875-1946

Rev. E. B. Watkins   1875-1906
Rev. L. R. Paterson 1907-1939
Rev. W. H. Wade   1939-

LESLIE RIMMER PATERSON M. A. (Oxon), The Vicarage, Woodend Lane, Speke. Born in 1866. He was vicar of All Saints Speke from 1907 to 1939.   His first wife Catherine (Katie) born 1865, died in 1913 aged 48 years. He married Ada Swift of Blacklock Hall Farm.   Ada was the daughter of Robert and Sara Swift. She was the organist in Speke Church. There were three children from this marriage, Josephine, Lois, and Stella.   In Miss Watts Will of 1921 he is listed as one of the executors, and was given £1000 in the will, a personal bequest.

All Saints Church Speke (1922)

The Font

Within the entrance of the church is the font made of Caen stone. As holy water was only blessed at certain seasons and had to remain in the font, a lid was necessary to keep it clean. The lid is of carved oak. The baptismal water was drained to the Garden of Rest. This is the font in which I was baptised in 1922.

Proceeding up the main aisle the first window on the right is dedicated to Frederick Ball Watkins, the first vicar of Speke. The window features St. Werburgh, patron saint of Chester Cathedral, to which diocese Speke once belonged. He is shown holding a representation Chester Cathedral, while St. Chad, patron saint of Lichfield, holds an image of Lichfield Cathedral.

Following on in the second window are the English saints, Alban, George and Edmund. This window is in memory of John Le Gendre Starkie who died in 1908. He was cousin to Miss Watt and son of John. P. C. and Ann Charlotte Starkie.

The third window is in memory of Leslie Rimmer Paterson, second vicar of Speke. The window portrays Saints Andrew, Peter and Helen who are connected with the history of the Church of Scotland.

On the right of the Altar is the window in memory of Ann Charlotte Amelia Starkie and shows Christ in the arms of his mother. St. Ann, mother of the Virgin is on the left, and St. Elizabeth, mother of John the Baptist is on the right.

The plaque on the right wall of the sanctuary is in memory of Katherine the first wife of Leslie Paterson who died in 1913 aged 48 years. Her ashes, with his are buried near the altar steps.

The east window is dedicated to the glory of God in memory of Miss Watt's parents. Adelaide Watt died at Kinross in Scotland on August 8th 1861 aged 23 years, and Richard Watt died at Cowes in the Isle of Wight, on December 9th 1865 aged 30 years. The centre panel shows the Annunciation, the crucifixion and resurrection of Jesus and the ascended Jesus on the throne. The two geometrical windows each side depicts the Blessed Virgin Mary in blue and the Holy Spirit

122

in red. Three smaller windows bear the signs for alpha on the left and omega on the right, with I .H. S. (Jesus Christ Saviour) in the centre. All the saints look in the direction of Jesus on the cross, accompanied by the words *Thou didst open the kingdom of heaven to all believers when thou hadst overcome the sharpness of death'*. The windows, when erected, cost £203.

On the altar below, the Rev. L. R. Paterson introduced brass candlesticks in 1912 and a brass cross. Mrs. Starkie Miss Watt's aunt gave the green frontal of the altar.

To the left of the altar is the window dedicated to Adelaide Watt. The window depicts the Resurrection; in the picture is Martha, in the centre, bearing oil and Mary the mother of James, with Salome, who went to anoint the body of Jesus at the tomb.

Miss Watt was cremated at Anfield Crematorium in 1921. A stone flag with an inscription covers the chamber.

The pulpit is of carved oak and Wrexham stone and cost £58.

The organ up until 1939 was a pipe organ with a hand blower. This required a boy to sit by the organist and work the handle to keep the air going through the pipes. It is recorded in the Speke Parochial Annual of 1938 that Cyril Coates an ex-member of the choir had undertaken the important office of blowing the organ. At a meeting on March 1st 1938 a report on the condition of the old Grey and Davidson Organ was given. It had been in the church from 1876 under the care of Messrs Henry Willis & Son. Considerable improvements and expenditure had taken place in 1907. As the organ by now, in 1938 required a further expenditure of £100 or more, Messrs Willis advised the alternative of buying a new organ at a cost of £975. This was not agreed. It was decided that an electric organ should be purchased. The one chosen was 'The Everett Orgatron' obtained from Messrs J Smith & Sons' at a cost of £420, minus an allowance of £75 for the old organ.

To the side of the pulpit is the new organ screen; this was erected in memory of James and Ellen Peacop of Speke Town Farm. The new electric organ was purchased in 1939.

The north stained glass window is thought to be dedicated to James Sprott. Clayton & Ball installed it at a cost of £128. It depicts four parables. The first is of the Good Samaritan, the second is the Parable of the Bridesmaids, the third is the Parable of the Talents, and the fourth is that of the Prodigal Son.

There are three phosphor bronze bells, weighing 4 cwt, 5 cwt and 6 cwt respectively. These were made and installed by John Taylor of Loughborough, they date from 1874 and cost £170. These bells were rung every Sunday until the outbreak of World War II in 1939. I was one of the bell ringers from 1937 to 1939.

THE NEW CHOIR VESTRY

At a meeting of the Church Council on the 10th January 1939 the contract was signed for the new vestry, according to the plans of Mr H Dodd. These plans had been submitted to the Council on the 14th November 1938 and had been accepted, after having been approved by the Bishop. The main contractor for this work was to be W. Whitty & Sons. The contract was to start on the 2nd January 1939, and to be completed by the 21st May 1939, (at a total cost of £875.3s.0d). On the completion of this vestry the choir would then have proper accommodation. There would also be room available for small meetings and provision for cupboards for storing church property.

New Choir Vestry (1939)

In addition to this the church would regain the seating space in the transept. This space had been used as a Choir Vestry, since 1907.

During her life, Miss Watt showed great interest in the church and its parishioners. At her death in 1921, in her will dated 23rd May 1918, she left £1000 in trust to the Church. This was invested between 1927-47 in War Stock at 5%.

The electoral roll for 1928-29 shows 129 men, 119 women, (209 residents, 39 non-residents which is a total of 248).

It is recorded in the Speke Parochial Annual for the year 1929 that the attendance at the Church Council Meeting had been on each occasion 11, 7, 8, 8, 7, 9, and 8.

Under financial business it states that due to the sale of the major portion of the estate of Speke, the trustees would not be able to continue their subscriptions as in the past.

This contribution was based upon 50% of the total contributed by the rest of the parish. The trustees declared themselves glad to subscribe one sum of £15, stating *"This sum to be applied by the Vicar as he thinks fit, and is to cover their whole subscription"*. It should be noted that during the years 1935-39 their subscription was increased to £25 and a donation of £5 was received from Mr. R. F. S. Hewson.

The total income for the church in the year 1929 was £99.2s.5½d with a balance for the year of £13.13s.11½d, and for the year 1939 an income of £160.10s.1d, with a balance for the year of £2.1s.2d.

In November 1938 the Rev W. H. Wade arrived to take up his post as the first curate of Speke.

THE POOR AND SICK FUND IN 1939

This is a Fund for the relief of the sick and of anyone who for some reason is in need of the church's helping hand. It comes from the offertories made at the early celebrations, except in those cases when the whole day's collection is devoted to some particular purpose. The total in 1938 was £4.8s.0d added to this sum the balance from 1937 from which only £1.19s.6d had actually been expended. Thus a sum of £6.14s.1d remains in the Vicar's hands to meet any cases that may arise in 1939.

At a meeting on January 10th 1939 it was decided to discontinue the publication of the Speke Parochial Annual after the 1939 edition. The Church Council at this time expressed their desire to develop a monthly news magazine called the *Speke Messenger*.

By the 31st May 1939 the electric lighting had been installed.

THE VICARAGE, WOODEND LANE, SPEKE

In 1937 the Vicar L. R. Paterson wrote in the Church Parochial Annual that the building of 500 houses in the near neighbourhood of the Church raised the question of the position of the vicarage.

When the vicar was instituted in 1907 the house and garden (then called the 'Slades') provided a good residence for the purpose of a vicarage in a scattered country parish. The house was used pending the provision of a more conveniently situated house to be built near the Church. The vicar became the first resident incumbent of Speke, at a nominal rent, and the 'Slades' became known as the vicarage, although it remained part of the Speke estate until, under the terms of the Will of the late Miss Watt, it was accepted, by the church authorities as a vicarage in 1922. With the consent of the vicar it became the property of the benefice. In a small country parish it did not matter so much that the vicarage was nearly a mile from the Church, for most of the people were also as far or further away. When the kitchen garden was laid out as a green the vicarage saw many happy meetings of the Men's Bowling Club and also the Women's Club. It was also the scene of other festivities and meetings. The population of the parish was so small that the inconvenience of the situation for the parishioners was not very great. Now, however, with a large population settled near the Church the idea of building a vicarage adjacent to the church should be considered and indeed taken up as soon as possible. The present vicarage is isolated by the new plan for Speke in the industrial area and quite outside the space allotted to the new residential township.

It would be a happy thing if the city authorities could join sympathetically with the vicar and the ecclesiastical authorities to build a suitable vicarage, which reflects the changed conditions of the parish.

It is interesting to note that the vicarage was put up for sale in 1938. It is recorded that an offer to buy the building and site for the purpose of a public house was turned down. It was decided that it would offend the instincts of many of the people of the parish. It was eventually sold and used as a bank. The new Woodend Avenue went through part of the vicarage garden. The curate used 72 Bray Road, Speke as his home in 1939. In 1940 this became the vicarage until the late 1940s.

The Vicarage

SPEKE TOWN STATION

The station was built and opened on the 1st July 1852. It was built on the Warrington and Garston railway and principally designed to carry coal to Garston Docks.   In 1864 a spur from Speke to Edge Hill was completed; Mossley Hill was a station on this spur.

In 1870 the Runcorn Railway Bridge was completed. This made it possible to link the Warrington and Liverpool line with Crewe. Speke was then on the main London to Liverpool line.

Mrs. Ada Paterson, wife of the Rev Leslie Rimmer Paterson, writes in the late 1920s, *'Mr. Beecham the stationmaster was a venerable looking man with a white beard. He used to keep trains waiting for us if he heard us coming. Often, we would be the only passengers embarking.'* The vicarage was just across the road from the station. On the 22nd September1930 the station was closed.

Speke Station, Speke Church Vicarage top left

'Station House', Thomas J. Bonner   Traffic Inspector (1920s)
Railway Cottage, Mr Beecham   Station Master (1920)

CHURCH SCHOOL

The Church School was built for Miss Watt in 1884 to replace tin cottages at 42-43 Hale Road, which had been used as a school. The Headmistress in 1928 was Mrs A. Bland. In this year the register records that there were 44 pupils.

Speke Old Church School

Speke Church School (1884)

On the school roll in 1934 there were 47 pupils. On March 10th the Upper School children went to town on the 10-20am bus. They spent an hour and a half at the Museum, had lunch at Lewis's and, in the afternoon saw Peter Pan at the Empire, for this the children each paid 6d. The School Games and Other Activities Fund met the remaining expense. On the 26th March, a certain F Hartley received a prize and certificate at St George's Hall for his R. S. P. C. A.

essay. The Diocesan Inspector, H. Lionel Gibbs paid the school a visit on the 4th September 1934. At a meeting of the school managers on the 28th they expressed their congratulations to the teachers and scholars upon the excellent report given. A school milk scheme was started on the 15th October. Each child to received a ½d bottle of milk each morning.

In the report for 1936, it stated that in the first half of the year, they had a wretched attendance due to various epidemics. During February more than half of the scholars were very ill, and summer holidays had almost arrived before they could return to normal attendance. This of course seriously affected the work in the school.

On July 12th fourteen of the older scholars had visited Lewis's to see a wonderful working model showing the production of petrol from coal along with the bi-products given off at the various stages. They then went to see Sir Malcolm Campbell's Blue Bird.

On September 29th Mrs. Paterson distributed the school prizes. Twenty-four children received prizes, provided by a grant from the Education Authority augmented by the managers and staff.

The prizewinners were N. Spann, A. Wyke, M. Farr, M. Whitehouse, N. Leadbetter, A. Farr, L. Dowell, M. Turton, R. Leadbetter, W. Johnson, E. Hulme, D. Johnson, E. Southern, U. Jones, D Latham, F. Hulme, F. Dooris, Denby. J., Hind. B. ,Norbury, F. Taylor, E. Dowell, and J. Lea. The 'Kitty Wilkinson' prizes went to L. Wignall and M. Green.

During the year of 1937, the dominant feeling was one of loss; because the school's beloved cricket field was given over to the aircraft factory. This field was at the end of Hall Lane by the school and church. They continued to use the field until it finally disappeared. In May a holiday was given to celebrate the Coronation. The Coronation party was held in the grounds of the vicarage in Woodend Road.

During the year 1937 the managers held three meetings, on the 16th July, 15th October and 13th December. These meeting were attended by managers of the school, the vicar and Mr. A. T. Powlett, agent for the owners of the school building and the trustees of Speke Hall. At the meeting on the 16th July they had before them a notice from the Liverpool Education Authority with regard to the provision of schools for about 2,300 children in the new Speke housing area. This notice gave them three months for any appeal on the part of the managers for the continuance of a church school in Speke. It was decided at the meeting on the 15th October that this matter should be left in the hands of the trustees.

It emerged from previous and later correspondence that the large sum of money required to adapt the small country school to fit in with the new scheme was not likely to be forthcoming either from the Speke estate, or from diocesan sources. Consequently it was decided that the school's only hope was to provide as many places as its accommodation permitted, until such a time as the new schools provided by the Education Authority were built.

In 1937 the trustees of the Hall wrote to the Parochial Church Council to inquire what the people of Speke would like to be done with the School and plantations after the Authority no longer recognised it as a School.

At a meeting of the Parochial Church Council on December 13th 1937 it was decided unanimously that the people of Speke would like the school to be given to the parish to fulfil the role of a parochial hall. This decision was sent to the trustees.

In their reply they said that they *"proposed to defer consideration of the future use of the building until the school has closed"*. By 1941 the building had become the parish hall.

In 1938 the pupils numbered 56 and in January 1939, there were126 pupils with three extra staff.

At a meeting of the managers it was decided that the school should close in May 1940. In August gasmasks were provided, this resulted in a holiday for the children, but in reality was a ghastly landmark.

In May 1940 the school closed and the pupils and staff were transferred to the new Stockton Wood School on the new housing estate.

GEORGE C. QUINT

George Quint was born in Aylesbury Buckinghamshire in about 1873 and came to Speke with his wife Edith, as far as I know, after the turn of the century. He was then in his late twenties or early thirties. They lived in one of the cottages at the end of Hall Lane not far from the North Lodge.

His duties as houseman in the Hall were to start work at 7am by stoking the central heating boilers in the boiler house (under the dog kennels in the back yard) and then the hot water boiler in the scullery. He then lit the range in the kitchen.

He went home for breakfast. On his return, he collected all the oil lamps that had been used during the night and cleaned and filled them (see the section on the lamp room). He then replaced the lamps in their respective positions in the

Hall. His next duty was to fill the buckets with coal and bring in logs for the fires. The rest of the day was spent cleaning and dusting the furniture or scrubbing the floors by hand. His working day ended after he had attended to the boilers at 10pm.

His working hours were from Monday to Friday, 7am to 5pm and 10pm to stoke the boilers, on Saturday 7am to 12 noon and 10pm to stoke the boilers. Sunday was free except for the boiler duty at 7am and 10 pm.

On Sundays he attended All Saint's Church, Speke and in 1917 became clerk and verger. His wife became church cleaner. He also found time to run a football team in the Liverpool League and had many other commitments within the church.

He had been something of a cricketer before he came to the Hall and always found time to have a game with us.

I remember him as a very kind and generous person. He gave us presents at Christmas, birthdays and when we went on holidays. This was usually five shillings each. In the early 1930s this was a great deal of money. It obviously gave him pleasure to give to us, as he had no children of his own. We could always go to him for advice on any project we wanted to carry out. He would encourage us and find us the materials to complete the job. He seemed to know something about everything.

When he was 63 years of age he retired from his duties as church clerk and verger and his wife retired as cleaner. In 1937 at a social evening held in the schoolroom he was presented with a wallet, and his wife a handbag, each containing a cheque for ten guineas.

It is interesting to note, that when the Quints retired, their positions in the Church were advertised in the Church Magazine as follows.

> THE VICAR TAKES THIS OPPORTUNITY TO SAY THAT THE POST WHICH MR & MRS. QUINT HAVE FILLED WILL BE VACANT AFTER EASTER AND THAT APPLICATIONS SHOULD BE MADE TO HIM FOR PARTICULARS. WITH THE DUTIES OF CLERK ARE INCLUDED THE VERGERS DUTIES, THE CARE AND HEATING OF THE CHURCH ALSO THE DUTIES OF SCHOOL CARETAKER. THE PRESENT SALARY IS AS FOLLOWS: - VERGER £15, CLEANING £13, CLERKS FEE £2-2s-5d (average for six years), SCHOOL CARETAKER £20, MAKING A TOTAL OF £50-2s-5d FOR THE COMBINED WORK.

George Quint retired from the Hall in 1940 and died on the 5th February 1945. He is buried with his wife Edith in the churchyard of All Saint's Church Speke. In 1919 his weekly wage at the Hall was £2-14s-0d.

George Quint (1926)

CHAPTER 9

FACTORIES, HOUSES, ROAD NAMES TO 1946

Before 1936 it would appear that there was apparently a laundry in Woodend Lane. This was run by Mrs. Mawdsley. It is reported in the Parochial Annual that, due to the closing of the Woodend Laundry, a charge would have to be made for the washing of surplices.

The only other workshop in the township before 1935 was the smithy. This was on the corner of Smithy Lane and Speke Church Road and was run by the Wyke brothers. As well as smiths they were wheelwrights and they carried out all the repairs on the farm machinery and shoed the horses. By 1939 the smithy had been converted into a library.

During the 1934 the first sod was cut, with due ceremony, for the inauguration of the first factory. The first factories were built in the region of Speke Hall Road and Edwards Lane on the land of Hale Road Farm.

On Monday, 15th February the vicar of Speke was calling at nearby Mill Brow when he became an uninvited member of a gathering on a small platform in a field of beautiful spring cabbages. The other members of the distinguished company were city officials led by the Lord Mayor, accompanied by the Dean of Liverpool, Sir Andrew Macalpine and Mr. A. A. Rowse of Rootes Securities Ltd.

The Lord Mayor proceeded to cut the first sod for the construction of the National Airframe Factory, which was completed in 1938 to assemble Blenheim bombers. Eventually a total of 2,443 aircraft were built until 1942.

The factory went on to build Halifax bombers. The first one took to the air on 17th March 1942. The eventual number built was 1,070 aircraft.

In 1940-41 the Lockheed Company set up a branch at Speke Airport to assemble Hudsons, which had been shipped, to Liverpool Docks. This facility was later to be known as No 1 Aircraft Unit.

NEW HOUSING ESTATES

The first housing estate to be built in the parish of Speke was called the Hollywood Estate. This was situated on the northwest side of the Hall at the Garston end of Banks Lane and was built about 1931. The new roads were called Winfield Road, Banks Way, Monks Way, and York Way. (Jimmy Lawless lived in one of the new houses in York Way. In the 1930s he was a great friend of mine and we would then have been 10 and 11 years old. We did everything together, he would visit the Hall at weekends and we would go fishing in one of the ponds for roach and other fish; sometimes we played in the woods, grounds or house. We lost touch with each other in the 1940s.)

As these houses are nearer to Garston than to Speke, the inhabitants feel themselves as citizens of Garston. This is despite the parochial boundaries, which compel them to have banns issued in Speke in accordance with the law.

It was during 1936 that a board appeared on the boundary of Hunt's Cross and Speke. This announced that a new housing estate was to be built. This estate on the Speke land was to be called the Garden City and was to comprise houses costing £525, with ground rent and rates of 19s.11d a week. Smaller houses were for sale at £475.

These houses were on Speke Church Road, and Speke Town Lane. New roads were made, School Way, Gerneth Road, Gerneth Close, Bray Road, All Saints Road, Greyhound Farm Road, Blacklock Hall Road and Rycote Road. This was the start of the Speke Housing Estate and by 1946 houses had been built on Hale Road, the new roads of Western Avenue, Linner Road, Goldfinch Farm Road, Sutton Wood Road, Stockton Wood Road, Tewit Hall Road, and Ramsbrook Close. The change continued. In 1937, 500 houses were built in the neighbourhood of Speke Church.

WHAT'S IN A ROAD NAME?

Looking at the names of the roads on the new Speke Estate built in the 1930s shows that they have been called after farms, woods, the church and houses.

Greyhound Farm Road: The farm was run by William Cartwright and was in the old Speke Town Lane. He was churchwarden for many years. The hostelry in Speke was called the Greyhound and was closed by Miss Watt in the late 1800s.

Blacklock Hall Road: This farm was run by Robert Heathcoat Swift and was at the end of the old Smithy Lane. He was lay representative and people's warden in 1929. He was also the father of Ada Swift who married Leslie R Paterson, vicar of Speke in the 1920s.

Tewit Hall Road: John Turton Critchley ran this farm; it was in Mill Brow off Hale Road and Oglet Lane.

Speke Town Road: Speke Town Farm was in Delf Lane and was run by James Peacop.

Goldfinch Farm Road: This farm was run by John Leslie Corlett and was in Hale Road.

All Saints Road and Church Road: These roads are named after All Saints Church Speke.

School Way: The Church School was in Church Road and was built for Miss Watt in 1884.

Stockton Wood Road: This road is named after the wood on the north side of Speke Hall.

Clough Road: This road is named after the Clough Wood on the south side of Speke Hall.

Sutton Wood Road: This wood was on Hale Road and Dungeon Lane.

Gerneth Road and Gerneth Close: The records show that before 1170 Sir Roger de Gerneth was a master forester, holding lands in Speke, Oglet, Whiston, Fishwick and Halton. He had the lands fee from William Earl of Ferrerd, *'as guardian of vert and venison in Lancashire Forests.'* His son Benedict succeeded his father as master forester. He was the last of the de Gerneths to hold that position, as he had no male heir, only two daughters Joan and Annora.

The interests of master foresters in Speke, however, became declined after Sir Roger de Gerneth granted the Manor of Speke *'in free marriage and without services attached to the grant'* to Adam de Molyneux of Sefton on his marriage to Annora, the daughter of Benedict.

Bray Road: John Norreys son of Sir Henry le Norris and Alice Erneys of Speke Hall married Millicent Ravenscroft of Bray, Berkshire. He was the founder of the chief Berkshire family of Norris and built Ockwells Manor House at Bray. In Burke's Peerage it states 'Sir John Norreys, KB, of Bray and Pattenden, Berks, Usher of the Chamber, Esquire of the body (also to Edward IV) and master wardrobe to Henry VI, Sheriff of Oxfordshire and Berkshire.

His son William, who was lord of the manors of Cookham and was knighted succeeded him but died at the battle of Stoke.

The vicar of Bray in the 17th century was Dr Francis Carswell who survived several reigns and various shifts in religions and political directions to become immortalised in the words of the English song *"whatever King shall reign, ill be the Vicar of Bray Sir"*.

It is interesting to note that the vicar of All Saints Church Speke in the 1940s was Rev. W. H. Wade who lived at 72 Bray Road.

Rycot Road. This road is called after a Manor House owned by the Norrises in the 16th century.

Henry Norreys, born in 1491, was a close friend of Henry VIII. He was accused, along with four others, of adultery with Anne Boleyn. They were tried and convicted in the Tower of London, beheaded and buried there along with Anne.

Henry Norreys, son of the above Henry was born in 1525 in Berkshire. After the death of his father he remained at court as a ward of Henry VIII. The King restored some of his father's land to him. He was ambassador to France in November 1566. In 1566 Queen Elizabeth I visited him at his home in Rycote and knighted him.

Known as Lord Norris of Rycote, after being summoned to parliament on the 6th May 1572, from the Queen he received he title 'Honricus Norris de Ricote'. He was granted new holdings in Berkshire and Compton. Queen Elizabeth who believed that his father, Sir Henry, was unjustly accused of having an affair with her mother restored all his lands to him.

The house at Rycote was burned down in 1747, but some remnants of it form part of the farmhouse, which now occupies the site.

St Michael's Chapel Rycote was the chief burying place of the Norrises and their descendants, till about 1886. Richard Quatremayne founded this chapel as a private chapel in 1449 for the Norris Family.

CHAPTER 10

THE INHABITANTS OF SPEKE TOWNSHIP
1920 - 1946

POPULATION

By 1929 the Census figures for the township of Speke amounted to 366. The work of the populace was generally on the land or in service on the estate. At this time the spiritual, cultural, social and recreational needs of the people were concentrated on the Church.

But by 1946 the population had increased to some 10,000 and the work was concentrated in the new factory estate. With an estimated population of 22,000, the new estate was by 1950 in a position to meet all physical cultural, and recreation needs.

The names of the families of the township of Speke listed in the Speke Parochial Annual of 1929 to 1940 as being on the Electoral Roll were as follows.

Andrews, Airport Manager *** Backshell, Shopkeeper *** Bailey, Chauffeur *** Ball, Farmer *** Barrow, Farmer *** Barton *** Bennet, Farmer *** Bland, Teacher *** Boult, Gamekeeper *** Blease, Organist ***Burn-Bailey, Companion *** Cartwright, Farmer *** Cleaver, Manservant *** Coates, Labourer *** Corlett, Farmer *** Corns, Labourer *** Crebbin, Gamekeeper *** Critchley, Farmer *** Crosby, Woodworker*** Crowther *** Dean, Gardener *** Dunbavin, Farmer *** Dutton Ellison *** Fowler, Estate Secretary *** Farr, Labourer *** Graves, Estate Agent *** Harland, Cowman *** Hartley *** Harrison, Farmer *** Hulme *** Lawless, Decorator**Latham, Gardener *** Lea *** Leadbetter, Farmer *** Lee-Steere, Companion *** Lewty *** Lowndes, Labourer *** Lucas, Labourer *** Lunt *** Marsh, Farmer *** Mawdsley, Farmer *** McIndoe, Farmer *** Moule, Police *** Nicholls *** Paterson, Vicar *** Peacop, Farmer *** Prescott *** Pye, Farmer *** Quint, Caretaker ** Roberts *** Simpson, Teamster *** Southern,

Gardener *** Spann, Teams man *** Sumner, Farmer *** Swift, Farmer *** Symonds, Gardener *** Taylor *** Travis, Office worker *** Turner, Farmer *** Turton *** Wade, Curate *** Whatmore, Custodian *** Whitehouse, Teamster *** Wignall *** Wilkin, Farm Bailiff *** Worral *** Wyke, Wheelwright *** Warren, Joiner *** Wynn *** Youd, Gardener.

The people listed as follows were part of the parish or township between 1920 and 1950 and in some cases before.

RICHARD and LIZZIE BACKSHELL: Richard married Lizzie Youd in the late 1920s and had a son William and a daughter Elizabeth Ann who was born 26th May 1934 and baptised in All Saints Church Speke on the 24th June 1934.

HAROLD JAMES and MABEL BLANCHE ANDREWS: Of Chapel House Farm, Liverpool Airport. Captain Andrews was appointed airport manager on the 6th July 1932.

P H HUGH and EVANGELINE BLEASE: Hugh was organist and choirmaster, at All Saints from 1929-1940. He was also the music teacher at Heath Road School, Garston. He died May 1964. He was organist at the Church for 21 years. They had a daughter Anne Mary, born 11th July 1934.

WILLIAM BAILEY (BILL): Chauffeur. Born on the 8th March 1882. See Chapter 3.

JOSEPH and ELIZA ALICE BARROW: Smallholder of Mill Brow. Eliza died on the 9th August 1931 and Joseph on the 12th January 1938.

MR. BALL:. A farmer of Chapel House Farm. This farm was at the Garston end of Banks Lane and was the first to be swept away to make room for the new airport in 1932. The house was used as the terminal and control tower for the new airport.

MR. JOE BALL: 62 Speke Town Lane. In 1936 he took over the duties as sexton. His main jobs were to take care of the Church and heating, ringing the Bell and keeping the Churchyard tidy. He was to be paid the usual verger's salary with the funeral fees and money for labour on the churchyard, which hitherto had been paid by the Council.

JOHN and MARY BALL: Of Speke Town Lane, whose daughter was Annie. Mary was the town's nurse and midwife.

ARTHUR. H. BARROW and JOHN BARROW: Of Poverty Nook, at the end of Oglet Lane. *'I don't know how it got its name, but no farm workers could be called affluent at this time.'* This is a quote from the notes of Ada Paterson.

ROBERT BENNET: Farmer of Speke Farm, Smithy Lane. This farm was always immaculately kept. He used to drive around in a gig drawn by a small strawberry roan pony. He was beautifully turned out and looked like King Edward VII.

MISS ALICE BURN-BAILEY: of Speke Hall. She was a companion to Miss Watt and was also a nurse at Garston Hospital. In Miss Watt's will she was left an annuity of £500 for life.

ALLAN and ANNIE BLAND: of 32 Hale Road, Allan was the postmaster and Annie the headmistress of the Church School.

GEORGE. BOULT: George Boult lived in one of the cottages on Oglet Lane. See Chapter.4.

ARRON HARRISON CARTWRIGHT: Farmer of Yew Tree Farm, the last farm on Oglet Lane before you arrived at the river. The Cartwright's were good kind people, always ready to give their time and money to the church. They had two sons and two daughters. He was people's warden of All Saints Speke 1934, vicar's warden and treasurer in 1936, 1938, 1939 and 1940.

WILLIE CARTWRIGHT: Farmer of Greyhound Farm, Speke Town Lane. He was churchwarden at Speke Church for many years and a very good man.

MISS CARTWRIGHT: Farmer of Goldfinch Farm, Hale Road. She was reported to be an excellent farmer. She was very stout but never missed walking to church on a Sunday morning. She was a very zealous worker. JOHN LESLIE CORLETT later farmed this farm.

ALBERT and MARGARET ELLEN CLEAVER: (nee Prescott) of 19 Speke Church Road. Margaret, before she was married was employed at Speke Hall as a maidservant. She was married in Speke Church in 1920.   After her marriage to Albert she carried out the laundering of the linen for Miss Watt, which Albert returned to the Hall on his bicycle.   Margaret died in September 1940. They had three children, Albert born 11th November 1921, Edith born 4th May 1924, and William Arthur born 19th February 1929, William baptised on the 31st March 1929 in Speke Church. In 1929 Albert and Edith won prizes at Sunday school in class 1.Out of 38 marks for good attendance, Albert gained 35 and Edith 33.

ROBERT LESLIE and ELSIE COATES: They had two sons Leslie and Eric both members of the choir in 1932.

ISAAC CORNS: Labourer, of the Cottage, Smithy Lane. He acted as dog-handler at all the shoots on the estate. They brought up their family in a three-roomed cottage. One of their daughters, Ethel married George Latham and had two girls who both married clergymen.

Mr. CREBBIN: Gatekeeper. A story was told by William Wyke son of Thomas Wyke who went to school with May the daughter of Mr Crebbin.

The story goes that if May and her mother were in when Mr. Crebbin opened the North Lodge gate for Miss Watt they would have to come out and bob a curtsy from the Lodge to her.

JOHN TURTON CRITCHLEY: Farmer of Tewit Hall Farm, Mill Brow off Hale Road and Oglet Lane. In 1931 he took over from his father, on his own account, a farm of 200 acres, with a large herd of pedigree attested friesian cows complete with a stock bull, whose name was 'Critchville Bonifacio'. The herd yielded 20,884 gallons of milk a year. He was churchwarden in the 1940s.

WILLIAM CROSBY: Lived at 6 Speke Town Lane with his wife Eliza, and had four children, Fred, John, Janey and Edith Alice. William worked at Rawlinsons in Window Lane, Garston for fifty years. He walked to work and back from Speke about four miles every day and was never late for work!

EDITH ALICE CROSBY: She left school in 1901. On the day she left school Miss Watt called to see her mother (ELIZA) and told her that she wanted Edith Alice to work at the Hall to live in and to start work the following day. She worked at Speke Hall for seven years, and hated every minute of it. The room she had at the Hall had one window and you had to kneel down to look through it. Edith Alice married Robert Wyke (son of Thomas Wyke) in 1917. (Graham Wyke son of Edith Alice and Robert gave this information to me in 1998). Graham died in 2001.

WILLIAM and ANNIE DEAN: William born 1880 was head gardener at Speke Hall up to 1930. Annie died on the 5th June 1927 aged 46 years. William died on the 20th September 1966 aged 86 years. They had a daughter Edith.

ERNEST and NELL FAZACKERLEY: Engineer who lived at 69 Hale Road, from 1942 to 1962. Ernest (known to the Scouts as 'Doc') was involved with the 16th Allerton Scouts from 1940 till 1950. During this time he was an Assistant Scout Master, Rover Scout Master and District Rover Scout Master. He was also very active in the church, serving on the P. C. C. and in 1948-49 becoming churchwarden. Nell was always supportive of all his activities both in scouting and church work. Each Sunday evening after church, a group of young people would be always welcomed at their home in Hale Road for discussions, a cup of tea and good company. These meetings started during the war from 1940 to 1945 and continued into the 1950s.

ELLEN. M. FOWLER: Mill Brow Cottages, off Hale Road. She was the youngest daughter of Mr. Graves of Sutton Grange. She had been left a widow with a boy and girl. Mrs. Fowler was the secretary to Miss Watt and carried on doing this work until 1939. For many years Mrs. Fowler and her daughter had taken charge of the washing of the altar linen and glass vases at Speke Church.

RICHARD GRACE: farmer. In the 18th century when Speke Hall was empty, there is evidence (provided by a decedent of the Grace family) that the Hall was used by members of the Grace family to keep cattle. It is alleged that, somewhere high up in the rafters, the name of Richard Grace has been carved into the wood.

RICHARD ASHBY GRAVES: Sutton Grange, Banks Lane. See Chapter.3.

MARY ANN GRIFFITHS: She was born on the 10th March 1888 at Longford, Kingsland Parish, Hereford and married in the parish church, Tattenhall, Staffordshire. She was a cook and had been at Berrington Hall, Leominster. She married Tom Whatmore on the 1st October 1916. He was then a private in the Kings Shropshire Light Infantry, but later to become Butler at Speke Hall. She died on the 1st April 1929 at Speke Hall.

MR. CUBBINS: Postman 1926-1936. Besides delivering the mail every morning to Speke Hall he would collect the morning papers and deliver them as well. On Christmas Day he had to do his normal duties, but when he came to the Hall he would get a glass of Port and a mince pie.

GEORGE AND JANE ANN HARLAND: of Home Farm Speke Hall. George died 15th July 1937 aged 56 years, his wife Jane died 8th January 1960 aged 79 years. He had moved to the Home Farm in 1929 with his family from Yorkshire. There was one daughter, Alice Mary and two sons, Leslie and Reginald.

REGINALD HARLAND: of Home Farm, Speke Hall. Born in 1919. Leading choirboy in 1932. Died in October 1998.

RICHARD STANLEY FITZGERALD HEWSON: He was born 1863 and died 1943. He was the son of Rev John Hewson and Sarah Watt. John Hewson was the vicar of Garston from 1869 to 1884. Richard was a first cousin to Miss Watt, and a main beneficiary in her Will. He negotiated with the National Trust in 1943. In 1943 he was living at 7 Somerhill Court, Holland Road, Hove.

JOHN IRELAND: of Speke Town Lane. Died 2nd October 1949 aged 91 years.

JAMES LATHAM: of Heath Cottages, Speke which was on the land of Blacklock Hall Farm. The Latham family had twin sons, Jimmy and Alfie. They were as alike as two peas. Jimmy was the church organ blower in 1920. James was a gardener at Speke Hall and became head-gardener from 1930 to his death on 12th May 1937 aged 65 years. Delia his wife died on the 31st July 1928 aged 62 years.

JAMES and JEANNE LAWLESS: York Way, Hollywood, Garston. They had a daughter Myrtle and son Jimmy. Jimmy was a friend of Tom Whatmore and visited Speke Hall at weekends in the 1930s. He was a member of the Speke Church choir and 6th Allerton Scouts Garston at this time.

MISS JANET LEE-STEERE: Speke Hall. She was the companion to Mrs. Smithson, and was an active member of Speke Church. She died in 1938 in Scotland.

EDMUND and MAGGIE LOWNDES: of 8 Baileys Lane. Edmund was a labourer at the Mount Pleasant Farm, Baileys Lane. Their son Cyril was a member of Speke Church choir in 1932.

CHARLES and JESSIE LOWNDES: Banks Lane. He was a labourer at Mount Pleasant Farm. They had four children, Harold, Fred, Margery, Winnie and Leslie. Charles died on the 3rd August 1955 aged 69 years and his wife on the 10th March 1973 aged 87 years. By 1934 as a result of the expansion of the Liverpool Airport, the family had moved away from Speke.

This is a copy of a letter sent to Tom Whatmore on the 14th November 1996, from Margery Lowndes, now Mrs. M Williams, who was born in 1915.

SPEKE 1920

A farming village on the banks of the river Mersey. It was self-contained having a very old manor house, and a moat round it. It had several farms, a smithy, wheelwright, and I believe coffins were made there. Church was a duty on Sundays, so we had a pleasant walk across the meadows. I believe she Miss Watt from the manor house was often seen riding her horse sidesaddle and was very keen to see everything was just right. The children enjoyed harvest time; they could play in the hay or take food and drinks to their fathers who worked really hard. Christmas was a happy time, you could look forward to a present from the Church usually brought by the Vicar riding his old bike, and wearing his old cloak. If you were sick, a free nurse checked you over and if it was serious you were packed off to hospital. Life was hard but had some memories.

Margery Lowndes,
Now Mrs. Margery Williams

GEORGE L and MINNIE LUCAS: Sutton Grange Cottages, he was a labourer at Mount Pleasant Farm. They had three daughters, Dorothy, Gladys, and Judith and a son Fred. A boy called Ronald, who was brought up by the family as a brother to Fred, was in fact Fred's nephew. He had been an illegitimate son of Fred's elder sister Dorothy. The two boys, being of the same age, were thought to be twins! They were members of the Speke Church choir in 1932. Gladys married a Harold King of Garston. Judith lived in one of the estate houses at the Garston end of Banks Lane. (Mrs. Sheila Miller daughter of Gladys King supplied this information) (nee Lucas.)

LIZZIE. M. MAWDSLEY: Woodend Farm. After the death of her husband she carried on an efficient laundry business in order to support herself and her two sons. When the Woodend Laundry closed Speke Church had to meet a charge for washing surplices. The Church Council at a meeting on the 21st January passed a very sincere vote of thanks to Mrs. Mawdsley who had, for many years, given the surplices her own special care by having them washed, whenever required, free of charge. This had been a very valuable help to the church accounts every year.

GEORGE GIBBON MARSH: J.P. farmer of Mount Pleasant Farm, at the end of Baileys Lane, and Banks Road. This farmland was sold off to Liverpool City for the airport in 1932. He was a J.P. and gossip had it that his frequent stockyard fires were caused by revengeful characters who had appeared before the bench for poaching offences. He had a son Baker Marsh.

WILLIAM FROGGATT McINDOE: He became the tenant farmer of Home Farm, Speke Hall in the year 1929. He was then 22 years old. He married Mary Mardsley Peacop on September 26th 1934. They had two children, Roger and Ian. Ian in 1993 was still farming Home Farm. Ian died in 1996. Home Farm then passed to the National Trust and was opened to the public in the year 2000.

FREDERICK. J. and JEAN MOULE: of 25 Hall Lane, he was a policeman. They had a daughter Freda, who married Edward Hayes from Hale, a school friend of Tom Whatmore in the 1930s.

STEPHEN LESLIE NORRIS: Born 1859. Trustee of Speke Hall, in 1921.

REV. EDWARD JOHN NORRIS: Born 1860, he married Nina Catherine Stures and was Hon Canon of Christ Church, Oxford. He was one of the trustees of Speke Hall in 1921. He published a history of Speke Hall, in August 1923, (later revised in June 1935). It was called 'The Building of Speke Hall'. He died in 1937. His son was Thomas P. Norris.

THOMAS PILKINGTON NORRIS: Born 1892. He was the son of Edward John. He married Elsa Mary Tatham. In 1943, under the terms of Miss Watt's Will he inserted the name of 'Watt' into his name. He was one of the chief beneficiaries in this will. He was a frequent visitor to Speke Hall up to 1946, and negotiated with the National Trust in 1943. In 1950 his address was "The Hearth", Redbourn, Hertfordshire.

Dr WILLIAM FOXLEY NORRIS: Born 1859. (Dean of York) and was trustee of Speke Hall. 1921. He married Mary Blanche Pott.

MAJOR JOHN PERCIVIL FOXLEY NORRIS: Born 1886. He married Doreen Brabant Smith in 1914. He was a trustee of Speke Hall 1921. They had two sons Michael born in 1915, and Christopher. He died in 1925.

MICHAEL FOXLEY NORRIS: Born in 1915. In 1943 he became a trustee of Speke Hall. In 1950 he was farming in Africa. His later address is Sherborne, Dorset.

LESLIE RIMMER PATERSON: M. A. (Oxon), of the Vicarage, Woodend Lane, Speke. He was born in 1866 and was tragically killed in 1939 aged 73 years. See Chapter 8.

JAMES PEACOP: Farmer of Speke Town Farm, Delf Lane. He was born at Jericho Farm, Otterspool, where his family had lived for 200 years. He was a great judge of horses and acted as buyer to the Liverpool Corporation, whose horses were the pride of the City. He died on May 17th 1934, aged 67 years. His wife Ellen Mary had died on the 11th December 1929 aged 62 years.

JAMES PEACOP, Junior: In 1929 he was lay representative of Speke Church and he married Mary Weir Forrest on August 30th 1934. He was people's warden 1936-1939. His farm was taken over for factories in 1935.

RICHARD and NELLIE PEARSON: Home Farm Cottages. Richard was cowman at Home Farm, Speke Hall. Nellie died on the 1st July 1971 aged 64 years and Richard on the 4th April 1975 aged 69 years.

A. T. POWLETT: Of Powlett and Henshaw of Bath and Sons Solicitors. Agent and Trustee of Speke Hall estate from 1926 to 1943.

PETER, GEORGE, JOHN and MARGARET PRESCOTT: 19 Speke Church Road. Peter and George were keen members of the men's choir, bell ringers and members of the Speke Church football team that won the Woolfenden Cup plus gold medals in the season 1926-27.

PETER PRESCOTT and CISSIE WYNN PRESCOTT: Peter died 17th October 1962 aged 63 and Cissie died 14th September 1976 aged 69.

GEORGE PRESCOTT: married Mrs. EDITH MAY TRAVIS (nee WYNN) in 1935. They had a daughter Marjorie, born 8th June 1936. In 1936 George is listed as a member of the Church Council. He accepted the office of Bishops Courier and was commissioned at the Cathedral during that summer. By 1938 he and his wife had both become Couriers.

MARGARET PRESCOTT: Married Albert Cleaver in 1920. (See Cleaver.)

JAMES PYE: Oglet Farm. He came to the township of Speke from Aughton and married Miss Howard of Mersey View Farm. On the 27th of October 1921, he was unanimously elected peoples warden to succeed the late Miss Watt. He held this office until 1928, when at his own request he relinquished it. He died in 1936.

GEORGE CHARLES and EDITH MARY QUINT: 26 Hall Lane. They were both great workers for the church, George being the verger and Edith the cleaner. They gave up all their spare time to the church and parish. They retired from this work in 1940. George died on February 15th 1945 aged 72 years and is buried in All Saints Church yard, his wife Edith died on June 18th 1961 aged 85 years. See Chapter 8.

ALICE M ROBERTS married HARRY WOODWARD: on the 6th April 1929 at Speke Church. In 1922 Alice was a maid at Speke Hall

LEONARD ROSSITER: of Speke, Liverpool. He was born in Liverpool in 1926 and educated at Liverpool Collegiate. In 1943-45 he was a member of the 16th Allerton Scouts at Speke. He started work in insurance after leaving school. He was very keen on amateur acting. He became a well-known professional actor in the 1960s. He died in 1984.

ROY and ANNIE SIMPSON: 32 Hale Road. He was a team's man at the home farm Speke Hall in1929. He died on the 24th July 1957 aged 62 years.

CHARLOTTE SMITHSON (nee Starkie): She was daughter to Anne and John Starkie and cousin to Miss Watt. She was born in 1865. She lived at Speke Hall until 1926. During her life at Speke Hall she regularly attended the services at Speke Church. She died in 1938 in Scotland. Her companion was Miss Janet Lee-Steere.

WALTER SOUTHERN: 57 Oglet Lane. He was the son of Elizer Southern (nee Wyke). She died on February 15th 1912 aged 72 years. Walter died March 12th 1950 aged 79 years. He was a gardener at Speke Hall.

JOSEPH HAROLD SPANN: Teams man of Mill Brow, who died on the 12th September 1960 aged 53 years.

ANNE CHARLOTTE STARKIE (nee Hudson): (see Charlotte Watt) married JOHN P C STARKIE, of Ashton Hall Lancaster in 1861. She was widowed in

1888. She was aunt to Miss Watt. She died at Speke Hall in 1925. Mrs. Starkie's ashes were taken by T. Whatmore (butler at Speke Hall) to Ashton Hall, Lancaster for burial. They had a daughter Charlotte born 1865 (see Smithson) and a son John born in1863. She gave the entire altar furnishing to Speke Church.

JOHN Le CENDRE STARKIE: He was born 1863 and died in 1908. He was a cousin of Miss Watt.

HERBERT and EVELINE SUMNER: 20 Speke Church Road. They ran a general store from the house in Church Road. Herbert died on the 2nd May 1956 aged 70 years and his wife Eveline on the 5th November 1958 aged 71 years.

LEN and MARION SUTTON: 3 All Saints Road. They were both born in 1904. They came to live in Speke about 1938. In September 1938, Marion (known as Marie) started the first cub pack in Speke and she ran this pack until the 1970s. She was also an active member of the church until her death in 1992. Len always showed an interest in scouting, having been a leader before he came to Speke. He always came to camp with the 16th Allerton and, in 1944 came to help with the running of the group. In about 1954 he became Assistant District Commissioner for Scouts in Allerton, and was one of the most active and enthusiastic people in the starting of the 32nd Allerton Group in Speke. He was also one of the principal workers in the building of the new headquarters called Roger Hall, opened on July 5th 1958. He continued to be very active in scouting until he resigned as Assistant District Commissioner in August 1961.

He died in September 1962. Marion continued to work with the 16th Allerton Group and All Saints Church until she died in 1992 aged 88 years.

ROBERT HEATHCOTE SWIFT: Farmer of Blacklock Hall Farm, at the end of Smithy Lane. He was lay representative and people's warden in 1929. When he and his wife first came to Speke they lived at Hunt's Tenement in Dungeon Lane. They were the parents of Ada Swift who married Leslie R Paterson in the 1920s. William S Harrison later farmed Hunt's Tenement.

ADA SWIFT: Blacklock Hall Farm. Ada was the daughter of Robert and Sara Swift. She was the organist in Speke Church and in 1921 married the vicar Leslie Paterson. (See Paterson)

EDWARD SYMONDS: Oglet Lane, Speke. He went to Speke Hall as a young gardener in 1924. He married Nellie Evans on the 14th April 1934. By 1938 he had become the head gardener and remained at Speke Hall until he retired. He was then living in the North Lodge.

WILLIAM TRAVIS: married EDITH MAY WYNN on the 2nd October 1929. He audited the Speke Church Football Team's balance sheet in 1928-29. William died on the 4th November 1932 aged 32 years. By 1934 Edith was a member of the Church Council and on the roll of parochial electors. In 1935 she married George Prescott.

REGINALD S TURNER: Nurseryman of Dungeon Lane. He was vicar's warden and treasurer from 1929-1935. In 1936 a permanent memorial called the Turner Memorial was placed in the Church. This was a large prayer book, which replaced the original one, which by then was worn out. The cost of the book with its inscription was £5-1s-9d, which was readily sent in response to the appeal made in church.

REV. W. H. WADE and HETTY CHRISTINE: 72 Bray Road, Speke. Curate from 1938 to 1940. He became Vicar from 1940. Rev Wade known in the parish as 'Peter' became the Group Scout Master of the 16th Allerton Scouts from 1939. His wife Hetty started the 313rd Guides in 1939.

CHARLES WALKER: Hale Road. Charles and his family came to Speke from Garston about 1939. He joined the 16th Allerton Scouts about 1940, becoming a patrol leader and at 18 years an Assistant Scout Master. In 1944 he went into the forces. On his return in 1946, he started studying to take holy orders. By 1960 he had become assistant priest at the Mersey Mission to Seamen.

ELI JOHN WARREN: 16 Brunswick Street, Garston. He died on the 18th November 1935 aged 73 years. His wife died on the 26th September 1950 aged 87 years. See Chapter.4.

CHARLOTTE WATT: Born 1814 and died in 1891. She was the third daughter of Richard Watt III. She married Harrington Hudson of Bessingby, North Yorkshire in 1834. This was her first marriage and they had a daughter, Anne Charlotte, born in 1836. After the death of Harrington she married the Rev Arthur Fane, of Boyton Manor, Wiltshire and Aston Lancashire.

It is recorded in the *Liverpool Mercury* of Tuesday May 21st 1878 that Mrs. A Fane (Charlotte Watt), attended Miss Watt's 21st birthday on this date in Speke Hall. There are three windows in Bishop Burton Church dedicated to her by Adelaide Watt.

MARY WATT: Born 1817 and died 1881. She was the fourth daughter of Richard Watt III. She married Mr. J Sprott of Dunbar in 1834. They had a son and daughter. In 1865 he became the guardian and trustee of Miss Watt during her minority. The family attended Miss Watt's 21st birthday party.

ADELAIDE WATT: Speke Hall. She was born on the 20th May 1857. She was a woman of strong character, a woman in a man's world. She always wore clothes of a severe masculine cut and sometimes trousers. She was a real eccentric and for the time had quite advanced ideas, (including the habit of smoking cigarettes, cigars or a pipe). Her companion was Miss Alice Burn-Bailey. She died on the 21st August 1921 after a short illness. See Chapter 1.

ROBERT E WILLIAMS: Farmer of Edwards Lane. He had two sons, William and Edward. William married Dolly Rhodes daughter of George Rhodes of Hale. They had a farm in Knowsley. They had one son, John.

THOMAS WHATMORE: Speke Hall, Butler to Miss Watt and Mrs. Starkie from 1920 to 1926. He was the custodian of Speke Hall, from 1926-1950. He married Mary Griffiths in 1916. She died on the 1st April 1929. Tom died on the 20th November 1967 aged 87 years. There were two sons, Frank and Tom. See Chapter 1.

MARY WHATMORE: (See Mary Griffiths).

FRANCIS EDWARD WHATMORE: Speke Hall. He lived in Speke Hall from 1921 to 1946. He was a member of the choir 1932 to 1934. He was called up to the R. A. F. in 1940, being demobilised in 1945 with the rank of Warrant Officer, Air Gunner. He married Marguerita Edith Lomax of Garston on the 25th May 1946. They emigrated to Australia in 1958. Frank died on the 21st July 1985.

THOMAS WILLIAM WHATMORE: Speke Hall. He lived in Speke Hall from 1922 to 1946. He was an active member of the church, having joined the choir in 1932 at the age of 10 years. He became a Bell Ringer in 1937 and member of the parochial church council in 1940. He joined the 16th Allerton Group in 1940 as an Assistant Scout Master (to replace the Scout Master who had been called up to the forces.) He took over the running of the troop with the assistance of Ernest (Doc) Fazackerley and Charles Walker, until the return of the Scout Master from the forces in 1946.

Tom married Margaret Atkin of Garston on the 22nd April 1946. On the beech tree across the road from the orchard and picnic area are the initials of T. W., done about 1936. In 1938 at the age of 16 years he was apprenticed to a firm of electrical engineers. During the years 1940 to 1946 he was on war work with the Admiralty in Liverpool. In 1956 he became the manager of the company and by 1965 was one of the directors. During 1970 he left to become a manager of an electrical engineering company in Liverpool. In 1980 he joined an electrical company doing work in London as an estimator and contracts manager. He retired in 1987.

MOSES WHITE: Gamekeeper Speke Hall. He lived in the gamekeeper's house in Oglet Lane. By his first wife he had two daughters, Agnes, born 14th September 1879, who married William Bailey on the 4th March 1913 and Sarah; he also had two sons, Arthur and Harry. There were two sons Frank and Alfred born to his second wife. Frank was drowned in the pond in Stockton Wood just off the Walk. Moses was a big man with a heavy beard. He died on the 31st March 1914 aged 67 years. His second wife Ann outlived him and died on the 19th June 1926 aged 83 years.

FRANK WHITE: He was the son of Moses and Ann White, born in 1873. On his gravestone in Speke churchyard is the inscription *'Their son who was accidentally drowned while skating February 21st 1888 aged 15 years'*. This is the boy who was drowned in the pond just off the Walk at Speke Hall.

JOSEPH THOMAS and HARRIET ELLEN WHITEHOUSE: Hale Road. He was a team's man at the home farm, Speke Hall. Known all his working life as Tom, he died in December 1977 aged 90. His wife Harriet died on the 30th April 1937 aged 43 years.

GEORGE L. and SUSAN W. WILKIN: He was the farm bailiff of Speke Hall's home farm until 1929. On one of the beech trees at the corner of the orchard and picnic area, is carved the name of G. L. WILKIN, dated 1926.

THE WILLIAMS FAMILY: Farmers of Rose Farm, Woodend Lane, Hunts Cross.

HARRY WOODWARD: married ALICE ROBERTS on the 6th April 1929. In 1926-27 he was a member of the Speke Church football team that won the Woolfenden Cup and a gold medal.

GEORGE and ELIZA WYKE: of 7 Speke Town Lane, George was born in 1861 and died in 1933 aged 72. Eliza (nee Webb) was born in 1867 and died in 1955 aged 91. George was the oldest retainer on the estate at the death of Miss Watt and was given the job of steering the oldest horse (Turpin), which pulled the oldest wagon bearing Miss Watt's coffin to Church. They had 9 children, Alice being the eldest.

ALICE WYKE: She was the daughter of George. She was born in 1901 and died in 1964 aged 63. She was a ladies maid to Miss Watt and Mrs. Starkie in the early 1900s. She married John Skinner in about 1925. Their daughter Hilda (born 1926) married John Williams and had a daughter Shirley in 1957. The following story told by her granddaughter. The story is that she and another maid would sneak up to Mrs. Starkie's room, pinch her Turkish cigarettes and smoke them. Nothing was ever said, although Mrs. Starkie must have become suspicious the smell alone.

Another story told by the granddaughter is that while her grandmother was in hospital with housemaid's knee, Miss Watt said, that there was no reason why she could not do the sewing even if she was laid up. She sent her sewing to Alice.

THOMAS WYKE: lived at 10 Speke Town Lane with his wife Ellen and their eleven children, Robert, Leonard, Ashton, Fred, Harry, Frank, Arthur, Alice, Nelly, Jessie and Edith. Thomas was a wheelwright and ran the smithy and wheelwright's business at the smithy at the village end of Smithy Lane. Two of his sons, Frank and Arthur, worked with him at the smithy.

The Anvil from this smithy is now in the porch of All Saints Church, Speke.

In the early nineteen forties the smithy was turned into the local library and was later demolished.

ROBERT WYKE: married Edith Alice Crosby in 1917 (see Crosby) and they had two sons Robert and Graham. Graham was born in June 1925 and died on Monday 9th April 2000, aged 75 years at a meeting of the Parish Church Council of St Michael Garston; he had been churchwarden for 15 years.

FRED WYKE: He was killed in the First World War. His name is on the Speke church war memorial.

LEONARD WYKE: He worked at Speke Hall between 1910-14 as gardener, groom and handyman. This was his first job after leaving school. One day he was sent to meet Miss Watt at Garston Station with the pony and trap. Having brought Miss Watt back to Speke Hall, he then should have changed the trap for the luggage-cart in order to collect Miss Watt's luggage from the station. Instead of doing this he returned to the station in the same trap to pickup the luggage and upon his return to Speke Hall he was seen by the steward Mr. Ashby Graves and immediately sacked for failing to change carts.

WILLIAM and FANNY WYNN: They had three daughters, Edith May, Annie, and Cissie. See Prescott.

WILLIAM YOUD: North Lodge, Bailey's Lane. His wife was called Sarah; she died 30th May 1934 aged 59 years. They had two daughters', Lizzie (see Backshell) and Annie. The latter became matron at Garston Hospital in 1934. During Miss Watt's life he would go up to the estate in Dunbar Scotland, to look after the horses.

ANNIE YOUD: North Lodge. She was a matron in Garston Hospital.

CHAPTER 11

ORGANISATIONS and SOCIAL ACTIVITIES

Speke Church Football Club, in the year 1926-27 won the Woolfenden Cup and gold medals. In the 1928-29 season they were in the Liverpool League, but found it very hard to win matches. Mr. J Peacop provided a ground. George C Quint ran the team and also organised social events in aid of the team.

In the balance sheet of 1928, the receipts were £32.1s.0½d with an expenditure of £20.10s.4½d. It is interesting to note some of items of expenditure.

	£ - s -d
League Fees	£1.2.0
Footballs and Bladders	£2.14.9
Shirts and Knickers etc	£5.9.7
Referee Fees	£4.13.4
Lime	6.3
First Aid Bag	6.6
Boots Chemist	7.2
Grants to Injured Players	£2.0.0

The balance for the year ending May 13th 1929 was £11.10s.8d. I cannot remember when the team closed down but I do remember going to watch their matches in the early 1930s.

Speke Church Football Team (1929)

The club ran its usual Boxing Day Social in the schoolroom in 1929, but the attendance was not up to the standard of past years. Maybe it had been the lure of wearing fancy dress that made the gathering so successful in the past. However, those present had a very happy evening.

In 1929 the vicar writes that the two Parochial Socials had much the same result as the year before. The one, in January, was a pleasant gathering, but too small in numbers to be financially successful (only 11½d was paid into the Balance Fund towards the usual advance for prizes). This left the old fund too poor to afford its usual contribution to the cost of the church annual and not very well able to advance money for prizes again.

When the time came to arrange the All Saints' Day Festival, the Church Council found that the Bible class had not resumed its meetings and there was no committee. It was decided to arrange the Social on new lines and an executive committee undertook all the arrangements. There were some generous promises for the prizes; help came from a Conjurer, Mr. Ernest Lee with songs and Miss Dorothy Cartwright with recitations. Mr. H. Blease kindly played the piano for the community singing, dancing and songs, so the expenses were practically reduced to the cost of refreshments. 134 tickets at 1 shilling (10p) each were sold and on November 6th, in a crowded room, we had a most enjoyable evening. A Cinderella Social was held at which Speke people past and present met in pleasant intercourse. This formed part of the celebrations connected with the church at the time of the All Saints Day Festival.

When the arrangements for the All Saints Day Social were being discussed, the happy thought sprang to mind of having a children's party on the day before. This would take the place of the pleasant Ascension Day gathering at the Vicarage, postponed in 1929 owing to infection in the School. Thus it was decided that, on the 5th November, a bonfire party should be held. An unforeseen spoke was put in the wheel of the bonfire site, but Mr. R. H. Swift and Mr. T .T. Critchley readily came to our help. The latter provided a site in a field opposite to the Greyhound and the former laboured hard to redirect the flow of materials and remove what had already been dumped on the usual field. All went well. A good tea, a good bonfire and some fireworks were enjoyed. The only thing not so good was the weather. Never-the-less we all enjoyed ourselves in spite of it.

In 1939 Speke Church Girls Club was beginning a new era and the hope was that before long, it would have a large membership of enthusiastic girls, under the leadership of Mrs. Wade. The Girls Club was originally formed for girls of 14 and over to be held in the vicarage every Thursday at 7.30pm. It had been felt for some time that the vicarage was not the most convenient place, for many girls lived in the centre of the parish. It was therefore, decided to change the venue to the Church School on a Friday at 7.30pm. It is reported in the Speke Parochial Annual of 1939 that *Many happy evenings have been spent in sewing and playing games, and the club worked hard for the Garden Sale and also on the day itself. A friendly spirit had been the keynote of all meetings.*

The Speke Church Women's Club. This was formed in April of 1939 with a view to bringing the women of the parish together in the fellowship of the church, and providing them with a time and place for meeting each other for work and discussion. There was a membership of 34. They had done much useful work during the previous year, raising £45 for the new organ fund. They also helped with the Garden Sale in July. In November they welcomed the Rev and Mrs. W. H. Wade to the Parish with a tea party. The Club had a ladies guild and they made themselves responsible for the care of the church.

In 1940 The Church Boy's Club was started. This club met in the Church School on one evening a week. The Association of Boy's Clubs supplied them with equipment. They had parallel bars, trapeze, rings, springboard, box and mat, boxing gloves, and medicine ball. It had an attendance of about 30 boys and was led by the Rev. W .H. Wade.

Mrs. Hill of 85 Rycot Road, as Brown Owl, and Miss Corrin as Tawny Owl, started the Brownies.

16th ALLERTON SCOUT GROUP, SPEKE

Mrs. Sutton started the cub pack; on the 1st September 1938 it met in the Church School, later in the church hall.

Cub Pack (1942)

Mr. Frank Bozie who was also Group Scout Master of the 1st Allerton, and District Scout Master started the Speke Scout Group. Recruiting commenced by a march round the roads of the estate led by the band of the 1st Allerton Group. This took place on the 1st September 1938. It was designated as the 16th Allerton Scout Group.

They met, to begin with, in Gregory's factory in Woodend Lane (now Metal Box Factory). By 1939 they were meeting in one of the farm buildings of Woodend Farm, Woodend Lane. In 1940 after the Church School had closed they met in the then church hall. In 1939 the leaders were.

Group Scout Master	Rev. W H Wade
Scout Master	William Burton
Assistant Scout Master	William Jackson
Assistant Scout Master	Thomas W. Whatmore

In July 1941, 41 Boys and 6 Officers camped for one week at Brynbach Nr Denbigh, North Wales. This was the first camp run by the 16th Allerton. Other camps were held in the years 1943 to 1946, all at Brynbach, with an average of 40 scouts at each camp.

In 1941 Bill Burton and Bill Jackson were called up for military service with the R.A.F. and did not return until 1946.

The Group continued until 1946 under the leadership of the following:

Group Scout Master	Rev. W H Wade
Scout Master	Thomas. W. Whatmore
Assistant Scout Master	John Ernest Fazackerley

Scout group (1942)

During these years the following notable events took place.

In 1942, the pantomime "Robinson Crusoe" (seven performances). The production of the pantomime started on the 22nd January 1942 and was supposed to run for 3 performances. However because of the great demand for tickets, a further four performances were arranged and given. The boys of the scout group played all the parts, both boys and girls. The cast in order of appearance were:

Joe Painter by Patrol Leader J. Bate
Polly Perkins by Second A. Day
Billy Crusoe by Patrol Leader G. Homan
Robinson Crusoe by Patrol Leader A. Holhouse
Capt. Scuttle by Patrol Leader C. Walker
Mrs. Matilda Crusoe by Scout McNally
Tom Bowline (1st Mate) by Scout R. Andrews
Singing Sam (the Shanty Man) by Scout J Ball
The Chinese Cook by Patrol Leader E. Fazackerley
Able Seaman Clark by Scout F. Day
Man Friday by Scout J Harding
And the Cannibal King by Second A. Hall

The chorus of seamen, sailor girls and cannibals were played by: Patrol Leader A. Biggs, Patrol Leader F. Mason and Scouts J. Guy, K. Tinsley, J. Richardson and J. Cumminngs.

In the finale scene the leaders of the group made an appearance:

Assistant Scout Master J. E. Fazackerley represented the Army. The Navy by Troop Leader Carruthers. The Royal Air Force by Scout Master Tom Whatmore. A scout by F. Mason, a guide by J Francis, a wolf cub by T. Walsh and a brownie by G. Martin.

The producer of the show was Percy Haxell who was serving at that time with the R. A. F. at Liverpool Airport. (Percy was a scout from Poole, Dorset)

1942, June 27th, Garden Fête:

This garden fête was run by the scouts in aid of the Speke Communal Drainage Scheme. The sum of £50 was raised.

The fête was held in the grounds of the old vicarage in Woodend Lane. The delightfully wooded grounds were dotted here and there with numerous stalls of every variety. On the extensive lawn two ponies were kept extremely busy conveying children around the grounds. Also on the lawn were facilities for badminton, table tennis and skittles. The mothers of the boys served ices and minerals.

Among the features was an ingeniously constructed "Chamber of Horrors" in the cellars of the old vicarage, recalling the past activities of a late tenant known as "Meat Hook Mike".

The boys of the troop were responsible for the individual stalls.

The afternoon festivities were completed with an impromptu concert given by the boys on the green and in the evening a flannel dance was held.

1944, First King Scout, Ernest Fazackerley:

Ernest became Speke's first King Scout with the coveted possession of the green and yellow all-round cords and first class certificate.

16ᵗʰ Allerton Cubs (1945)

July 1944 Rover Scouts started. With J E Fazackerley as leader.

The Rover Crew was formed on June 7th 1944. The first members were:

J. E. Fazackerley, (leader), T. W. Whatmore, C. Walker, W. Stacey, D. Thompson, E. Roberts and D. Brown. The first Rover camp was in July 1945 at Brynbach, Denbigh, North Wales.

1946: The purchase of Maycrete Hut for the Scout Headquarters. This was purchased from the Ministry of Defence for the sum of £80.

GUIDES (313rd LIVERPOOL)

In January 1939, a Girl Guides unit was started under the leadership of Mrs. Hetty Christine Wade, wife of the curate the Rev. W. H. Wade. On the 5th February 1944 the guides presented a pantomime called **Robin Hood**. There were five performances. The producer was Betty Wallace, with help from Mr. Hughes, Mrs. Greenhalgh, Mr. Tom Whatmore and Mr. Whitehurst.

Scouts and Guides at
Speke Hall (1943)

Guide Pantomime (1944)

CHAPTER 12

TRANSPORT

During our early years at Speke Hall, our only means of transport round the estate was by bicycle or pony and trap. In 1929 when my mother died, horses pulled the funeral carriages and hearse. These were usually black, with black harness and accoutrements.

If we had to go into Liverpool, it was by single-decker bus. This bus came through from Warrington via Hale Road and Hall Lane to the North Lodge. It was here that the bus would stop and we were able to get on board.

The route was then along Bailey's Lane to Speke Road, Garston, St Mary's Road, and on to Liverpool. The fare for this journey was sixpence plus 1penny return. The penny was the fare between Speke and the end of Bailey's Lane. The fare was sixpence from the beginning of Speke Road and Liverpool.

Alternatively we could go to Liverpool by riding our bicycles into Garston where we would leave them in one of the shops in St Mary's Road and then board an electric tramcar. The route number of the tramcar was '33' and the fare was one penny.

By the middle of the 1930s, after the estate was taken over by the Liverpool City Council, a regular double-decker bus service was available. When Bailey's Lane was closed we had to walk from the Hall to a stop on Speke Hall Avenue, a distance of one mile.

Tom Whatmore Senior (1950)

CHAPTER 13
THE NEARLY COMPLETE CIRCLE

I started my life on the 11ᵗʰ May 1922 in the bailiffs' house on the Home Farm, then in 1924 I moved to the West Lodge, (the West Lodge has long been demolished) and in 1926 I moved into Speke Hall east wing. After 20 years in the Hall, in 1946, I moved away from the Hall to get married (on April 22ⁿᵈ). My brother Frank also moved away in 1946 to get married (on May 25ᵗʰ). My father (left) stayed on at the Hall until 1950 to help with the opening of the Hall to visitors. He retired in August of that year.

Tom and Peggy Whatmore (1946)

Frank and Rita Whatmore (1946)

161

After 40 years I returned to the Hall, now in the care of the National Trust. In May of that year I took a party from the Mossley Hill History Group on a visit on one evening to the Hall and the administrator, David Mounce, met us. He accompanied us on a tour of the house and was so interested in my description of the house and rooms that I was invited to talk to the stewards at a party which was given as a 'thank you' for their services to the trust during the 1st year. This was on the 3rd and 4th October 1986.

I had been already talking to groups on "My Life At Speke Hall" (my first ever talk was to the Mossley Hill History Group in 1984). These activities re-established my connection to the Hall.

After I retired, I returned again to the Hall as a day steward volunteer at the request of David Mounce. This was in May 1987 and very soon I became the steward day organiser. I am still Friday Organiser in 2009.

All this connection with the Hall still does not complete the circle for me, as I would like to see the east wing open to visitors. At present my bedroom is a kitchen in a flat used by one of the Hall's officers.

In January 2008 it was mooted that the East Wing would eventually be opened to visitors. A group of volunteers would be involved in helping to plan this opening. I was delighted to help in any way I could in this enterprise.

Only one room is open at present (May 2008), namely the room that was the maid's sewing room. It gave me a great amount of pleasure to contribute any knowledge I had of past time in the east wing. The Whatmore family is well represented in this room.

So, starting my young life at Speke Hall, returning as a volunteer and lecturer, and being involved in the east wing nearly completes the circle for me. The circle cannot, for me, be closed, until the East Wing is completely open to visitors.

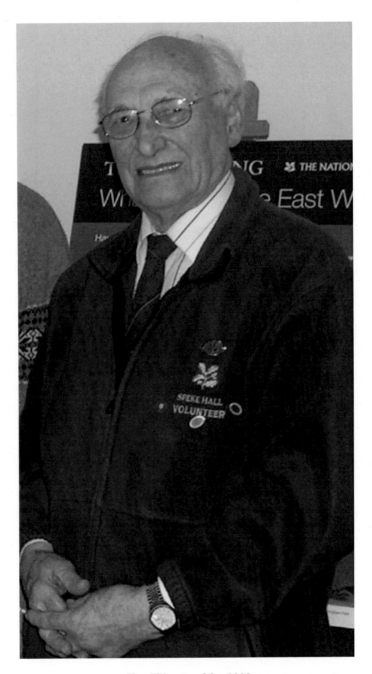

Tom Whatmore, May 2008

ACKNOWLEDGMENTS

Merseyside Aviation Society Ltd.

Speke Hall, Notes and Information for Official Guides (November 1948) by Harold. J. Andrews, Warden.

Speke Hall by Herbert Winstanley (1919)

Speke Church Parochial Annual 1930-38.

Action Stations by David. J. Smith.

Notes written by Mrs. Ada Paterson and photographs.

All Saints Church Speke 1988, by Vivien Rive Kennils.

Home Farm photographs from Ian McIndoe.

Frank Bailey, son of William Bailey, Chauffeur Speke Hall.

Notes written by Shirley Williams (Alice Wyke's Granddaughter).

Notes written by Mrs. Ruth Rimmer (Thomas Wyke's Granddaughter).

Notes written by William Arthur Cleaver 1996.

The National Trust (Speke Hall).

I wish to thank: Belinda Cousins, Assistant Historic Buildings Representative, The National Trust, and Ernest Smith, M.A, author of *A History of Mossley Hill Parish Church* and *A Short History of Mossley Hill*, for reading and making many useful comments and suggestions for the book of 1993.

Also to John Boston for his many suggestions and amendments to the Third Edition of 2009.